HORACE'S ROMAN ODES

A Critical Examination

MNEMOSYNE

BIBLIOTHECA CLASSICA BATAVA

COLLEGERUNT

A. D. LEEMAN · H. W. PLEKET · C. J. RUIJGH

BIBLIOTHECAE FASCICULOS EDENDOS CURAVIT

C. J. RUIJGH, KLASSIEK SEMINARIUM, OUDE TURFMARKT 129, AMSTERDAM

SUPPLEMENTUM SEPTUAGESIMUM SEPTIMUM

CHARLES WITKE

HORACE'S ROMAN ODES
A Critical Examination

LUGDUNI BATAVORUM   E. J. BRILL   MCMLXXXIII

HORACE'S ROMAN ODES

A Critical Examination

BY

CHARLES WITKE

LEIDEN   E. J. BRILL   1983

ISBN 90 04 07006 0

CONTENTS

PREFACE

I should like to thank the Horace H. Rackham school of Graduate Studies of the University of Michigan for making it possible for me to conduct research in Italy for this work, and for much help in the preparation and publication of it . My thanks are also extended to the staff of the Apostolic Library of the Vatican. I also express my gratitude to Professor John H. D'Arms for his warm hospitality in 1979 as Director of the American Academy in Rome, where much of the present work was carried out, and likewise for his imaginative support as chairman of my Department. Finally, my thanks to Baoyu, Canyon, Yogi and Aileen Gatten for making my tasks easier.

Ann Arbor, Michigan
7.II.83

CHAPTER ONE

HORACE AND THE ROMAN ODES

To embark upon a study of Horace's Roman Odes, the first six odes of his third book of lyrics, and so-called from their patriotic themes and address to Roman citizens, is to enter a well-worked terrain. For centuries students of Latin lyric have addressed themselves to the myriad facets of these six texts, and have also, sometimes brilliantly, attempted a study of their entirety.[1] To offer yet another work concerned with these poems implies that something new can be said about them, some novel meaning or interpretation be imputed to them or ostensibly elicted from them. Yet it might also be useful to assemble a study of the Roman Odes which, while offering no startling re-assessment of their import as a whole, might nevertheless raise certain questions about the Roman Odes in light of new perspectives opened up by modern literary criticism on the one hand, and new awareness of the dimensions and strategems of Roman political art on the other. Such a study might enable one to experience these poems more fully as a twentieth century reader, as well as suggest ways whereby the text organizes itself in accord with principles more

---

[1] For the coining of the term "Roman Odes" to mean Horace, *Odes* III.1-6, reference is usually made to Theodore Mommsen's "Festrede" in *Sitzungsberichte der königlich Preussischen Akademie der Wissenschaften*, (Berlin, 1889), pp. 25ff. But the term occurs earlier in F. Curschmann, "Die Römeroden," *Horatianis*, (Berlin, 1887), pp. 43-56. Among numerous studies one may note F. Klingner, *Die Römeroden: Studien zur griechischen und römischen Literatur* (Zürich, 1964), pp. 333-352; R. Heinze, "Der Zyklus der Römeroden," in *Vom Geist des Römertums* (Stuttgart, 1960), pp. 190ff., a reprint from *Neue Jahrbücher für Paedagogik* 5 (1929), pp. 675ff.; Eduard Fraenkel, *Horace* (Oxford: Oxford University Press, 1957), pp. 260ff.; G. Pasquali, *Orazio lirico*[2] (Florence, 1964), 649ff.; Carl Koch, "Der Zyklus der Römeroden," *Neue Jahrbücher für Antike und Deutscher Bildung* 2-3 (1941), pp. 62ff.; Hans Opperman, "Zum Aufbau der Römeroden," *Gymnasium* 66 (1959), pp. 204ff.; Victor Pöschl, "Poetry and Philosophy in Horace," *The Poetic Tradition* ed. D. C. Allen and H. T. Rowell, (Baltimore: The Johns Hopkins University Press, 1968), pp. 47ff., especially pp. 58ff.; L. A. Moritz, "Some 'Central' Thoughts on Horace's Odes," *Classical Quarterly*, n.s. 18, (1968), pp. 116ff., especially pp. 125ff. Studies of the individual poems have also been undertaken by Fraenkel and by Steele Commager, *The Odes of Horace* (New Haven: Yale University Press, 1962). References to these two scholars will be noted in connection with the several Roman Odes. D. O. Ross, *Backgrounds to Augustan Poetry* (Cambridge: Cambridge University Press, 1975), pp. 139-152, also addresses some comments to the Roman Odes. These have been termed "the finest use to which these methods [of Ross: viz., to move from small philological points to wider literary implications, with sensitivity to nuances of tone and style] have ever been put"; J. E. G. Zetzel, "Gallus, Elegy and Ross," *Classical Philology* 72 (1977), p. 250. R. Heinze, *Vom Geist des Römertums*, p. 213, thought the Roman Odes the most discussed work of Roman literature.

familiar to an Augustan audience than to our own times. Without arrogating to itself the claim of definitiveness or even total novelty save in the application of methods not hitherto invoked for the examination of Horace's poetry, such a study as the present one might also validate certain modern critical approaches to an ancient text.

The idea of civic poetry in lyric form is foreign if not repugnant to a modern Western audience. For us, the lyric is essentially private, even an overheard statement made by the poet in relation or reaction to some vision or experience of his world to which his words give us access. For the ancient world, such a conception of lyric poetry would have been embarrassing or even incomprehensible, as were certain aspects of Catullus' highly personal and unironic verse for Horace. Classical Greek usage had restricted *melé* to poems sung to musical accompaniment, in distinction to iambic and elegiac verse, and in contrast to non-narrative and non-dramatic poetry. Horace's poems, which open up Latin lyric to the wealth of Greek meter and subject, were indeed lyrics but not designed for singing,[2] rather they are lyrical by virtue of their meters, subjects and forms. The term lyric as modernly used is non-generic and descriptive, denoting poetry presenting the artist's image in relationship to himself, fusing concept and image in sound. For the Greeks as for the Romans, the lyric poet, in varying ways and with increasingly complex developments, spoke not only for and to himself, but for all who could hear him and heed him. There was a clear place for the lyricist in Greek literature; one need only think of the political statements of the Aeolian poets reflecting tension between the received oligarchic traditions and newer ideas. The Roman audience for Horace's three books of *Odes*, published as a unit in 23 B.C., would have been prepared through awareness of Greek antecedents to understand that lyric poetry addressed to public concerns existed as a recognizable form. Further, their own literature had provided, through Ennius' *Annales* and Lucilius' books of satires, to name but two of many, the examples of poets who addressed civic concerns, if not in lyric, at any rate in verse. An Augustan audience would experience increasing manipulation of its attention also by means of political statements made on coins, and in civic art. Finally, an atten-

---

[2] *Pace* A. Bonavia Hunt, *Horace the Minstrel* (Kineton, Warwick England, 1969), an idiosyncratic work devoted to this thesis. It is the contention of E. Poehlmann, "Marius Victorinus zum Odengesang bei Horaz," *Philologus* 109, (1965), pp. 133ff., that the Odes were to be recited, not sung. On Horace's Alcaic meter see J. P. M. Blackett, "A Note on the Alcaic Stanza," *Greece and Rome*, second series 3, (1956), pp. 83f.; J. Hellegouarc'h, "Observations stylistiques et métriques sur les vers lyriques d'Horace," *L'Information litteraire* 18, (1966), pp. 66ff., especially p. 74. For rhyme in Horace, see O. Skutsch's remarks in the *Bulletin of the Institute of Classical Studies* of the University of London 11, (1964), pp. 73-78.

tive reader of the first two books of odes preceding Book III would have noticed recurring expressions of civic concern as early as the second poem of the first book. Here at the outset of his lyric corpus Horace presents the city, indeed the state, lashed by civil strife, attacked by the gods, and imploring heaven for the fulfillment of the rôle Augustus is to play in resolving conflict. This second poem of the collection follows one wherein the poet presents himself and his life in contrast to others engaged in diverse pursuits: in other words a forecast of III.1 and 2, the poet's self-representation (but without reference to a patron) and the exultation of civic *virtus*.

Other themes occur in common between the preceding odes and III.1-6, the Roman Odes.[3] The reader of Horace's *Odes* has received through reading other lyric in Greek, and more specifically the poems preceding the Roman Odes themselves a quantity of data enabling him to deal effectively with both civic lyric and with the complex themes and manifold levels of interpretation found in the cycle. Instead of approaching the Roman Odes through this preceding aggregation, however, it is purposed to study them directly after a brief look at the political scene of around 23 B.C. It is not the intention of this study to attempt a reconstruction of the perceptions and expectations of an "original audience," since such an effort is doomed to fall short of its hoped-for goal inasmuch as each act of reading a literary text is a fresh creative act. Nevertheless, some awareness of the milieu of this poem-cycle, both in the process of reading through the *Odes* to reach it and in the historical world of poet and audience, is desirable.

Horace's political and intellectual stances have been long and well charted through means of his *Epodes, Satires* and *Odes,* as well as through the *Epistles* and fourth book of *Odes* subsequent to *Odes* I-III. His relationship and attitudes in regard to Augustus, who figures so largely in the Roman Odes, may be taken as indicative of his complex evolution of ideas about the new Roman state coming into being after a century of civil war.[4]

---

[3] E.g., *Odes* I.12, 14, 35, 37, and II.1. See also H. C. Toll, "Unity in the Odes of Horace," *Phoenix* 9, (1955), pp.153ff., especially pp. 156ff. F. Fontaine, *Enchainement et groupements des poèmes dans l'œuvre lyrique d'Horace,* Liège, 1941-42; Mémoire de licence); H. Haffter, "Zur Komposition horazischer Oden," *Wiener Studien,* N. F. 10 (1976), pp. 199ff.

[4] For what follows on Horace and Augustus, see Chester G. Starr, "Horace and Augustus," *American Journal of Philology* 90 (1969), pp. 58-64. See also his "Virgil's Acceptance of Octavian," *American Journal of Philology* 76 (1955), pp. 34-46; see also M. Bourgeois, "Horace, Serious Reformer," *Classical Bulletin* 31, (1955), pp. 62ff.; A. La Penna, "La lirica civile di Orazio e l'ideologia del principato," *Maia* 13, (1961), pp. 83-123, 209-245, 257-283; A. La Penna, *Orazio e l'Ideologia del Principato,* (Torino, 1963); G. Williams, "Poetry in the Moral Climate of Augustan Rome," *Journal of Roman Studies* 52, (1962), pp. 28-46 on the *Odes*; and P. Grimal, "Les Odes romains d'Horace et les causes de la guerre civile," *Revue des Etudes Latines* 53, (1975), pp. 135-156.

It seems clear that Horace gave Augustus his full support only for a relatively short time, and that the time of publication of *Odes* I-III, 23 B.C., marked a time when the tide of commitment began to ebb away. Horace's youthful feelings of social and political concern can be seen in his fighting in the army of Brutus and Cassius as a tribune: a commitment referred to with pride several times in his poetry and once in the Roman Odes themselves.[5] Further, Horace's aristocratic rather than democratic bias appears often: e.g., *Odes* III.1.1ff. alone show his distrust of the masses. After the wreck of his world at the end of the civil war, Horace buys the post of *scriba quaestoris* and works in Rome, meeting Octavian's minister of internal affairs, Maecenas, in the early 30's, when Octavian was struggling to end the Roman revolution and reestablish a structured society for Rome. From probably late 38 B.C. on, Horace had Maecenas' support and encouragement as well as a limited access to Octavian. As his success through the 30's and early 20's grew and order was restored to the Roman state, Horace's gratitude and support for Octavian's program (the success of which resulted in Octavian taking in 27 B.C. the name Augustus) can be seen in the first three books of *Odes*, including specifically the Roman Odes.[6] Later the ever-present shadows of doubt and pessimism grow deeper; Horace turns increasingly to philosophy, especially Stoicism, and enunciates, principally in his *Epistles*, growing concern for the tone of contemporary society.

The pessimism about the Roman order at the end of the Roman Odes, III.6.46-48, and the prominent attack on materialism there and the use of the term *libero* in III.5.22,[7] show that Horace's aristocratic contacts and biases, and his complicated character, increasingly content to assign to Augustus mere conventional flattery unlike his deep and authentic expressions of sincerity in *Odes* I-III, did not allow him to continue for long to present Augustus and the state's well-being as coterminous.

The context of the Roman Odes is no longer solely that of 23 B.C., however. There is an interaction of text and reader, both contemporary to the poet and contemporary to ourselves, that must be examined. The modern reader is not interchangeable with an ancient, nor can he imaginatively or scientifically recreate and animate his ancient counter-

---

[5] *Odes* II.7; *Satires* I.6 and 7; *Epistles* I.20, 23 and II.2, 46ff.; *Odes* III.4.26.

[6] E.g., see Fraenkel (*op. cit. supra* n. 1), pp. 260ff.; Laura O. Sangiacomo, *Le "Odi Romane"* (Rome, 1942). For the religious dimension of Horace's friendship with Maecenas, see K. Eckert, "O et praesidium et dulce decus meum," *Wiener Studien* 74 (1961), pp. 61-95.

[7] The adjective *libero* in III.5.22 is not used in connection with materialism, to be sure; but words like *liber, libertas* and their derivatives appear only once again in *Odes* I-III: see III.24.12, this time on materialism; their frequency mounts from the first book of *Epistles* on; see Starr, "Horace and Augustus" (*supra* n. 4) p. 63.

part's text. Rather, the modern reader is handicapped, in respect to the ancient audience, by not being able to read many Greek lyrics and many works of Roman literature now lost that no doubt had a bearing on Horace's Roman Odes, and helped create a context for reading them. To counterbalance this deficiency the modern reader has (potentially at any rate) the experience of more lyrics in other non-classical languages, a radically different idea of civic poetry (often bad political oratory made worse by pretensions of meter) and a lot of critical baggage that probably had no counterpart in the ancient reader's mind. Likewise, it would be idle to pretend that we have Horace's text of the Roman Odes. We do not; rather, we have what is very likely a better approximation of this text than we have for many ancient writers. Yet even the 336 lines of the Roman Odes exhibit several critical cruces, and the very division of the text into six odes is open to question. For the purposes of this study, the text followed is that of Friedrich Klingner's Teubner edition.[8] But one must bear in mind constantly that, although the correlation between Teubner text and Horatian holograph is, in these poems, of a very high magnitude, the fit is not totally perfect. The "text" brings its own problems, minor but real and substantive enough, just as does the "audience," both ancient and modern. The sole supposition made with any degree of confidence in the following pages is that the text we study is in Latin, and that we know a good deal, but not everything, about how to read that language; and that the reader has worked his way to the Roman Odes at the outset of Book III by reading the text seriatim.

---

[8] *Horatius: Opera* ed. F. Klingner[5] (Leipzig, 1970; unchanged from the third edition of 1959).

CHAPTER TWO

THE *ORDO LEGENDI*

The first four lines of the first Roman Ode have often been regarded as a prologue.[1] But to what? The plural *carmina* has been adduced to mean the whole cycle, viz., III.1-6. Yet the first poem has no addressee, and this has been taken to imply that those Roman Odes with an addressee, such as poem 4, lines 1-4, poem 6, lines 1-4, and even poem 3, lines 69-72, may constitute other elements in the cycle with the result that III.1.1-4 serves to introduce only poems 1-3, or the third book of *Odes* as a whole. A vexing element in these questions is that after reading the whole collection of Books I-III in order we note that the third book of *Odes* contains a poem, III.24, which has no addressee, and which is obviously an adumbration of the Roman Odes, a transitional stage in the evolution of the poet Horace's political thought from the pessimism and even despair of the early days (such as seen in the sixteenth *Epode*) to the relatively positive stance in III.1-6. This twenty-fourth poem of the third book, "Intactis opulentior," in the second Asclepiadean meter, develops in linked form the themes of greed and luxury presented in III.1, and the theme of sexual demoralization in III.6.[2] So in a sense it too could be one of the *carmina non prius audita* of III.1.1-4, especially if *non prius audita* be taken to mean "not previously heeded," implying "songs here renewed," as has been suggested.[3] Another attractive idea is to link Books II and III by poem twenty of Book II, making it serve as a prologue to III.1-6 as well as epilogue to the second book.[4] A great deal of study needs to be directed to the problem, probably ultimately intractable, of how divisions between books of poetry would have been perceived by an ancient audience, and of how we might expand our

---

[1] See e.g., Friedrich Solmsen, "Horace's First Roman Ode," *American Journal of Philology* 68 (1943), pp. 337-352, especially p. 337. For a denial of a connection between strophes one and two of III.1 and what follows in the next ten strophes, see L. Amundsen, "The 'Roman Odes' of Horace," *Serta Eitremiana* (Oslo, 1942), p. 7; E. T. Silk, "Cicero and the Odes of Horace," *Yale Classical Studies* 13, (1952), p. 150 n. 6 regards the opening of III.1 as a proemium.

[2] F. Solmsen, *op. cit. supra* n. 1, pp. 343-347.

[3] Edmund T. Silk, "Towards a Fresh Interpretation of Horace, Carm. III.1," *Yale Classical Studies* 23 (1973), p. 132.

[4] E. T. Silk, "A Fresh Approach to Horace, II.20," *American Journal of Philology* 77 (1956), pp. 255-263.

awareness of these joinings as links as well as boundaries.[5] How much are we to keep in mind that the end of Book II, viz., II.20, looks ahead to III.1-6 as soon as we have got to the end of the sixth poem of the third book? How much weight should we attach to the uncontestable fact that we may observe at the end of another book, I.35.18, the *Necessitas* of the beginning of the third book, III.1.14? Poems III.1-6, II.20 and I.35 are in the Alcaic meter; does the poet so arrange his corpus in Books I-III that ends and beginnings look toward each other, or is this but fortuitous?[6]

There would seem to be enough to observe in connection with III.1-6 without moving to other texts in the first three books of *Odes* to raise problems of ordering. Yet these questions are symptomatic of our lack of understanding (and ancient copyists' and scholiasts' lack of understanding) of the significance of poem boundaries and indeed of book boundaries.[7]

A set of detailed observations about sequences of poems in the same meter needs to be made in order to see how Horace has assigned to the Roman Odes a prominent place in the corpus of the first three books of his *Odes*. (We should also bear in mind that when he issued these as a unit in the form of three papyrus rolls in 23 B.C. he very likely had no plans for adding a fourth book, which appeared only in 13 B.C.) The data are cumbersome to present and are hence reiterated from different perspectives, but it seems essential to have a full-scale discussion in order to form a basis for judging Horace's artistic program for the Roman Odes as a whole before embarking on detailed interpretation of each ode.

In five places besides III.1-6[8] does Horace put poems of identical meter next to each other in the first three books of his *Odes*. These places

---

[5] On the level of the individual poem and in connection with modern literature, see Barbara Herrnstein Smith, *Poetic Closure* (Chicago: University of Chicago Press, 1968); for Horace, see P. H. Schrijvens, "Comment termine une ode? Etude sur les façons différentes dont Horace termine ses courts poèmes," *Mnemosyne* 26, (1973), pp. 140-159.

[6] Gordon Williams, *The Third Book of Horace's Odes* (Oxford: Oxford University Press, 1965), p. 23, avers that such seeking for the poet's organizing principles is "a waste of time." His commentary is a most useful discussion of the individual poems themselves, and I am much indebted to its observations. On the other side see R. A. Sarno, "Autotelic Argument for Unity in the Roman Odes," *Classical Bulletin* 42, (1966), pp. 49-53. The basic problems of the Roman Odes' organization are set forth in G. Duckworth, "Animae Dimidium Meae: Two Poets of Rome," *Transactions and Proceedings of the American Philological Association* 87 (1956), pp. 299ff.

[7] Some important MSS of Horace (e.g., A, E, R, Blandinus, also Porphyry) tend to link III.2 and 3, 3 and 4, 4 and 5, 5 and 6. Preliminary work on certain MSS of Horace in the Vatican Library and the Biblioteca Laurenziana in 1979 indicates that the whole problem of the transmission of the Roman Odes as continuous text deserves close scrutiny, which I hope to undertake elsewhere.

[8] One should note that if one ignores a book boundary one has in II.19-III.6 a sequence of eight poems in Alcaics.

are I.16 and 17 (Alcaic meter); I.34 and 35 (Alcaic); II.13, 14 and 15 (Alcaic); II.19 and 20 (Alcaic); and III.24 and 25 (second Asclepiadean). Like the Roman Odes, most of these constellations are in the Alcaic meter. Poem III.24 has long been regarded as earlier in date of composition than the Roman Odes, with a political context of 28/27 B.C., the period also suggested plausibly for III.6, in relation to Augustus' rebuilding of the temples in his sixth consulship. Poem I.35 has been assigned to 26 B.C.[9] Themes common to III.24 and III.1 and III.6 have been persuasively demonstrated: greed and luxury, III.1; sexual laxness, III.6.[10] Even on the lexical level similarities too close for coincidences exist, e.g., III.24.3 *caementis* and III.1.35, *caementa;* III.24.5 *Necessitas* and III.1.14 *Necessitas.* Hence it is reasonable to conclude that certain echoes of the Roman Odes are designed to await the attentive reader pursuing the poems of the third book in order, or, to put the matter in another way, certain elements of III.1 and III.6 recur toward the end of Book III, the whole collection of the *Odes.* Evidently Horace put the earlier compositions on either side of the cycle, elements of which, e.g., III.6 may have existed before the very idea of poem sequence. It should also be observed that Book III is divided at its center with Poem 16, addressed to Maecenas; poem 24 stands thus at the beginning of the second half of III.16-30, to be perceived as a unit because of the address to the patron at its outset.

Before turning to III.25, the metrical mate to III.24, let us examine the ways in which II.20 has been regarded as a prologue to the Roman Odes. Its forward-looking claims of greatness, its prophetic tone, its pointing to a new field of poetic endeavor, i.e., epic themes in lyric form, the Roman Odes themselves, the mystical autobiography, all have been adduced as elements in a "Bacchic overture" to the Roman Odes.[11] More observations, following this general line of thought but trying to go beyond it, can be made. If II.20, a public poem concerned with illuminating the status of the poet who is (in reading sequence) about to begin his Roman Odes (who has, in actual time, of course "already" written them when the audience has the edition of the three books at hand),[12] II.19 is a

---

[9] See G. Williams, *op. cit. supra,* n. 6, p. 128 and p. 62, and Bernard Fenik, "Horace's First and Sixth Roman Odes and the Second Georgic," *Hermes* 90 (1962), pp. 74ff. See also *Q. Horatius Flaccus Oden und Epoden* ed. Adolf Kiessling and Richard Heinze[9] (Berlin, 1958), *ad loc.*

[10] F. Solmsen, *op. cit. supra* n. 1, p. 346. On repeated words see W. C. Helmbold, "Word Repetition in Horace's Odes," *Classical Philology* 55 (1960), pp. 173f.

[11] E. T. Silk, *op. cit. supra* n. 4, p. 263. On the poet's metaphor of self as bird, see J. Tatum, "Non usitata nec tenui ferar," *American Journal of Philology* 94 (1973), pp. 4-25.

[12] These would consist of three papyrus rotuli in a box or bucket; see F. G. Kenyon, *Books and Readers in Ancient Greece and Rome*[2] (Oxford: Oxford University Press, 1951), p. 65.

private, personal experience with the god Bacchus, which poem or experience finds public expression in II.20. III.25, on the other hand, is the personal poem glossing, as it were, the longer and more public III.24. Are there points in common between these "personal" and "visionary" texts arranged in inverted or chiastic order?

Again, similarities too close to be accounted for by coincidence, especially in view of the difference in meters employed, can easily be discerned. Both poem groups have to do with Bacchus, to be sure, but even on the lexical level there seem to be deliberate correspondences: III.25.1f. says that the poet is "Bacche,... tui plenum;" II.19.6 has *pleno Bacche pectore.* III.25.6 uses *recens* of the poet's proposed subject matter inspired by Bacchus, and II.19.5 uses *recens* of the fear engendered in the mind of the poet who observed the same god. A link, at least one, exists also between II.19, the "preface to the prologue to the Roman Odes," if one may so call it, and one of these odes; III.4.49ff. mentions the threat of the Giants to divine order, and III.19.21ff. also mentions this *cohors Gigantum* (and Bacchus' rôle in its destruction; we may recall he was changed into a lion for this combat).[13]

Perhaps enough has been indicated, even in this compressed form,[14] to show that verbal parallels exist between III.24 and 25 and the Roman Odes on the one hand, and between II.19 and 20 and the Roman Odes on the other, with certain similarities also to be observed between II.19 and II.20 on the one hand, and III.24 and III.25 on the other. The significance of these conjunctions will be suggested after examining the relationship between the other Alcaic sequence, I.34 and 35, the Roman Odes themselves, and III.24 and 25.

The hymn to Fortune, the thirty-fifth ode of the first book, has been brought into discussion of the Roman Odes hitherto chiefly because it presents *Necessitas* and her spikes as part of the procession of *Fortuna,* and can thus be linked to the *Necessitas* appearing in III.1.14.[15] We note yet other parallels, perhaps more interesting intrinsically than the double appearance of a goddess or personification such as *Necessitas,* highly utilitarian as she is to such speculations as I.35 and III.1. These include the *volgus infidum* of I.35.25 and the occurrence of *volgaris, fideli* and *volgarit* in III.2.23 and 25 and 27 respectively, and the *volgus* of III.1.1; *Fides* in I.35.21 and an aspect of her in III.2.25 (*fideli* again); Caesar in

---

[13] Should one note the *asperum leonem* of III.2.11? Probably not.

[14] Parallel placements of these similarities could also be adduced, e.g., *recenti* in the first half of the second strophe of II.19 (line 5) and *recens* in the second half of the second strophe of III.25 (line 7).

[15] That *Necessitas* here does not equal death was the persuasive contention of E. T. Silk, *op. cit. supra,* n. 3, pp. 139-145.

I.35.29, and in III.3.11 (Augustus); the Eastern enemy of the Roman state, I.35.29ff. and III.2.3, III.5.3ff., and III.6.9. The themes of civil war and of moral decay are observed in I.35.33ff., and of course find resonant echoes in the Roman Odes, e.g. III.6.

A few parallels can be demonstrated between I.35 and those poems near the end of Book III that we have seen directly bearing on the Roman Odes themselves: the theme of moral laxity finds expression likewise in III.24, and the adjective *recens* is employed in III.25.6 (the fresh subject matter) and I.35.30 (the fresh military levy) as well as II.19.5 as already noted (the fear of the god Bacchus). In the Odes, *recens* is used elsewhere in III.30.8, III.27.43 and I.10.2; it may be fortuitous in III.25, II.19 and I.35 though the Bacchic context of III. 25 and II.19, as well as the Bacchus of III.3.13, tend to suggest otherwise. Unmistakable however is I.35.17f., *Necessitas/clavos*, and III.24.6f., *Necessitas/clavos*.

Carmen I.35 is, like II.20 and III.24, a public statement; its immediate predecessor I.34[16] is, like II.19 and III.25, a personal statement by the poet from which flow the subsequent poems, I.35 and II.20, and to which the preceding poem is referred in the case of III.24 and III.25. In the case of I.35, it stands twenty-three poems away from the onset of the Roman Odes. In the case of III.24 it also obviously stands twenty-three poems away from that cycle's inception. In the case of these poems the following diagram showing a certain chiastic order may prove useful:

ROMAN ODES

23 poems*	23 poems
I.35 (public; hymn to the god)	III.24 (public; power of evil)
I.34 (personal; power of the god)	III.25 (personal; power of the god)

*including II.19 (personal; power of the god) and
   II.20 (public; results of divine ecstasy)

The foregoing collocation of lexical similarities and thematic passages from poems in Books I-III of Horace's *Odes* suggests that III.1.1-4 is not precisely *the* introduction of the Roman Odes. The attentive reader, reading sequentially (an assumption examined below) will have seen the poet dealing with civic themes, and, more important, will have experienced, through the texts of II.19 and II.20 (the Bacchic grandeur of

---

[16] I.34 is linked to I.35 by E. T. Silk, *op. cit. supra*, n. 4, p. 260, note 3.

the poet's station) theme, function and outlook on the world highly similar to those of the Roman Odes. The first four lines of the first of these, then, function to introduce a *sacerdos* whose credentials are already established; an audience, not the general masses who can understand Latin poetry, but the new audience which this poet will, in large part through *carmina* III.1-6, create, and which has otherwise carefully followed the poet heretofore. These poems will be entirely original (*non prius audita* in that sense looking ahead to III.1-6), viz., epic themes in a lyric meter, and all too familiar but hitherto unheeded, with *non prius audita* looking backward in the reading sequence to such texts as I.2, II.1, etc., which address civic concerns, and, proleptically, looking to such poems as III.23, composed earlier and hence known through recitation to at least some of the readers of the edition of Books I-III in 23 B. C. but not yet encountered in the *ordo legendi*. [17] A new poetry for a new generation, by a new kind of poet-priest, not Orphic or Eleusinian, nor even the Bacchic priest implied by II.19 and 20, but *Musarum sacerdos*, the further particularization of the *biformis vates* of II.20.2f. [18]

Before pursuing inquiry into the Roman Odes themselves, something should be said about the processes of reading a collection of lyrics such as Horace's. It is one thing for the critic, using a text in codex form and armed with such aids as the *Lexicon Horatianum*[19] to turn quickly from the first to the third book of *Odes* in his search for correspondences that form a frame for the central Roman Odes. It is another for a reader, using *rotuli*, to unroll the panoramic sweep of the Odes on papyrus in serial order. The former can consider the text as a simultaneously present whole; the latter is bound by the *ordo legendi*, and so discovers the text at every moment. But only at the first reading, as it were; subsequently, especially in a culture attuned to reading and hearing as part of the same experience, and perhaps for skilful and highly competent readers at the

---

[17] By this is meant the order of the poems as published in 23 B. C. and as encountered in the rotuli of this edition. For aesthetic implications of the ordering, see N. E. Collinge, "The Publication Order of Horace's Odes," *Publications of the Classical Association* 52 (1955), p. 119 (a resumé).

[18] Bacchic elements predominate in *Odes* I.19.20, III.3.13 and 69 (cf. II.19.25f.) whilst Apollonian elements can be seen in III.4.4 and 21 and 69ff., (cf. II.19.29ff., both concluding strophes). On *Musarum sacerdos*, we should bear in mind that the Muses' cult at the Mouseion at Alexandria and at other Mouseia involved both worship and literary pursuits. These centers were presided over by a priest of the Muses, and existed from before the Hellenistic period. The Mouseion at Alexandria combines cult, religious feeling and literary activity with a presiding priest much as Horace shapes the opening of the Roman Odes; see P. M. Fraser, *Ptolemaic Alexandria* (Oxford: Oxford University Press, 1972), I. pp. 312-319, and L. Boesing, "Musarum Sacerdos: Anmerkungen zu Horaz, Carm. III.1.1-4," *Vergangenheit Gegenwart Zukunft* (Würzburg, 1972), pp. 42-53.

[19] Domenicus Bo, *Lexicon Horatianum* (Hildesheim, 1965). Another basic research tool is Lane Cooper, *A Concordance to the Works of Horace* (Cambridge, Massachusetts, 1916).

first encounter, the poems though encountered serially in locked order form an incipient totality as they are read aloud. Perhaps more easily than we, who are accustomed to ready reference to texts contained in the pages of a book rather than in the colums of a papyrus roll, the ancient reader after even one experience of *Odes* I-III could summon up through memory the similarities we have just ponderously recovered from that text.

It must be stressed that correspondences, these or others, do not constitute interpretation. The parallels adduced between the Roman Odes, II.19 and II.20, I.34 and I.35, and III.24 and III.25 are drawn to the reader's attention in support of certain artistic effects to which attention will subsequently be directed. However, it is essential both to bear in mind that interpretation is a critical activity different from observation, and that the process by which these parallels are assimilated by the reader of Horace is a question prior to any investigation of their function.

To a reader, as we must assume the ancient audience to have been, who experiences lyric poems as a collection, a whole, even "a book at a time," the order of these poems in their books is a register upon which the artistic ability of the poet may play. A famous example is the opening of Horace's first book of *Odes,* where nine different meters, in succession, a veritable virtuoso display, confront the reader with the language's first extensive production in Greek lyric meters. Here difference of meter makes the impact that eight poems in the same meter, viz., the Alcaic, makes at II.19-III.6. But can one go beyond sameness and difference as categories operating to arrange the collection? The first observation to be made in answering this query is that sameness and difference are not always constant. For instance, the difference of meters in the first nine odes of Book I are congruent with differences in subject matter: the poet's lyric stature, the stricken state in need of divine aid, the propempticon to Vergil, the right use of time, the poet capsized by love, to name (oversimply) the principal themes of the first five odes. The six Roman Odes, it must now be noted, perhaps exhibit sameness in a way unexpected by their modern reader: for the probably third century commentator Porphyry and certain manuscripts and scholiasts[20] the first six poems of Book III constituted a unit, an unbroken run of Alcaics.[21] Here sameness of meter shades into continuity and identity of text in a way unavailable

---

[20] *Supra,* n. 7.

[21] II.19 and 20, never apparently linked together, were separated from the Roman Odes since they occur before the MS explicit/incipit statements about Books II and III. For a similar linking of two poems in Catullus, see his *carm.* 65 and 66 in MSS O, G and R(V) and Wendell V. Clausen, "Catullus and Callimachus," *Harvard Studies in Classical Philology* 74 (1970), pp. 85 and 93f.

to modern literatures, deprived as they are of the boundaries exerted by meter and genre, and enslaved to the printed page's layout and format. Even though the modern reader and critic may have difficulty in following the swift changes in subject in the Roman Odes when they are perceived as six divisible entities, his ancient counterpart probably invoked the identity of meter (and evidently in some manuscript traditions the continuity of text as well) to contribute unity in which to ground his experience of the text or texts.

I have above suggested that III.1-6 are introduced by the sequence II.19-20 and framed by texts twenty-three poems away from the Roman Odes on either side, viz., I.35 and III.24, each with an antecedent or subsequent accompanying text. All but III.24 and 25 are in the Alcaic meter. The spatial terms used here, "frame," "side," "antecedent," "subsequent," need testing. It is my contention that reference to another artistic medium, that of the Roman historical relief, offers a helpful analogy in showing how these texts may be encoutered in both serial and recapitulatory, cumulative fashions, so that the reader is enabled to make interpretations and recuperate meanings carefully structured by the poet's texts into a relatively narrow range of possibility.[22] The plastic artist's medium of space, the sequence of, say, the unrolling scenes on the column of Trajan or of Marcus Aurelius, is the literary artist's medium of time: of time's sequence in reading the poems in the order ordained by opening a rotulus at the beginning and moving from poem one to poem two, etc. Yet we cannot fairly shackle an ancient poet into making recitations from his poems in so unvaried a fashion. It is to be sure speculation, but I trust a safe one, that poets often selected certain poems from their works, poems especially suitable to the audience, the occasion, the season, and other variables. Perhaps such recitations breaking from the order of the received (or to be received) text were read from individual sheets when not produced from memory, just as modern poets giving recitations often do not read their poems in an order determined by a printed edition. Now if we allow the poet to do this, we may also confidently, if provisionally, allow the same privilege of skipping,

---

[22] See Mario Torelli, *Typology and Structure of Roman Historical Reliefs* (Ann Arbor: The University of Michigan Press, 1982), pp. 119-120, 123 on the continuous narrative of cyclic columns; pp. 120-125 on the relations between continuous narrative and triumphal paintings, animated geographical maps, the recording of *acta publica* as *commentarii*, and the pseudo-narration of triumphal arches: all as distinguished from reliefs of the status or function type, such as the altar of Domitius Ahenobarbus. See also Inez Scott Ryberg, *Rites of the State Religion in Roman Art* (*Memoirs of the American Academy in Rome* 22, 1955), especially pp. 38-75. For a somewhat analogous approach to monuments and literature see H. T. Rowell, "Vergil and the Forum of Augustus," *American Journal of Philology* 62 (1941), pp. 261-276.

juxtaposing and omitting to a skilful and competent reader of the poet as well, just as the art historian may examine scenes of campaign, battle, sacrifice, etc., from a cyclic column not in the order of presentation but according to thematic or technical groupings. Once the tyranny of order established by the succession of poems is broken, we are free (if we work within sane and responsible limits) to create groupings of text that suggest new possibilities for interpretation, just as we have been able, all along, to examine individual poems without reference to their context in a sequence, a book or a collection.

That this process of regrouping is anticipated and facilitated by the artist can be seen in the great difference that lies between a corpus of poetry ordered by the poet himself, such as Horace's, and that arranged by a subsequent editor, working perhaps along mechanical principles with a collection frozen into premature arrangement through the death of the poet: for instance, the Catullan corpus does not and cannot be made to exhibit the features elicited here from Horace's lyrics in the first three books of Odes.[23] Here the ordering mind of the poet can be discerned.[24]

However, one major disadvantage accrues to such an unyoking of the poetic texts from the order imposed by the poet: one creates context for oneself rather than experiencing the context incontrovertably established by the poet, when one skips about from place to place in a collection as large as the *Odes*. To invoke once more the model of plastic art, it is as if one moved wilfully or even capriciously from scene to scene of the *Ara Pacis Augustae*,[25] "reading" them for their informational content, now gazing at the scene of Aeneas and the white sow, now at the historical personages of the imperial house, now at the small reliefs on the inner and outer left and right wings, the *lex arae* in visual form:[26] all are indeed

---

[23] W. V. Clausen, "Catulli Veronensis Liber," *Classical Philology* 71 (1976), pp. 37-43; J. F. G. Zetzel, "Horace's *Liber Sermonum:* the Structure of Ambiguity," *Arethusa* 13 (1980), pp. 59-127 shows great sensitivity to Horace's arrangement of the first book of *Satires*.

[24] *Pace* G. Williams, *loc. cit. supra* n. 6.

[25] Obviously closer in date to Horace than the columns of Trajan and of Marcus Aurelius, the *Ara Pacis Augustae* was voted in 13 B.C. and dedicated in 9 B.C. For photographs and bibliography, see Ernest Nash, *Pictorial Dictionary of Ancient Rome* (New York, 1961), pp. 63ff. The writer is indebted to Professor Inez Scott Ryberg for a detailed inspection of this monument in Rome some years ago, and to Mario Torelli, *op. cit. supra* n. 22, pp. 27-61.

[26] On the *lex arae*, an inscription prescribing for an altar the kind of animal sacrifice, use or omission of fire, days of sacrifice, etc., see Reisch in Pauly-Wissowa, *Realencyclopädie* 1B (1894) 1686-1687 ("Bestimmung der Altäre"). Torelli, *op. cit. supra*, n. 22, p. 36, interprets the frieze on the *Ara Pacis Augustae* crowning the parapet of the altar as a figured translation of the *lex arae;* I believe that a similarly functioning *lex* or prescription for use can be found in Horace's corpus of Odes I-III. With special reference to the Roman Odes, the poems I.34, I.35, II.19 and II.20 and III.24 and III.25 function perhaps as a

part of an artistic program, all indeed exhibit levels of significance in themselves. But unless placed in the context of orientation and order of experience controlled by the architecture, and its own topographical location,[27] these scenes remain random signs: beautiful, perhaps, but devoid of essential context, the ground for all competent interpretation, and therefore remaining solely self-referring. Just so with a monument as complex and far-reaching as Horace's first three books of *Odes,* or even the small world contained in the Roman Odes themselves. Each poem exhibits certain significances; from each poem interpretations can be competently recovered. But each poem has as part of its existence its placement in the whole poetic corpus, or at least very many poems of Horace (and other ancient poets) do.

Just as one's access to a figurative monument like the *Ara Pacis Augustae* with its historical reliefs was controlled by the architectural setting of the altar and its enclosure, together with the urban topography of the site, so too access to a book of poetry (*a fortiori* in rotulus form) was controlled by the order in which the poems were placed. However, just as when one has examined all of the *Ara Pacis Augustae,* for instance, its individual scenes cohere in a comprehensive mass, and can by imagination or by physically retracing one's steps, be brought once again to one's attention, so too a collection of poems once read, in the order presented by the poet, can take on a dynamic new property of being imaginatively re-ordered, and perhaps read or recalled not seriatim but selectively. What is important to remember first, however, is that for both monument and literature experience of the work is first regulated and only then freed from axial inspection in the case of a building[28] or in the case of poetic texts from the linear *ordo legendi.* Only badly designed buildings or monuments (or those, like Hadrian's Pantheon that seek to baffle and defeat the viewer's desire for orientation and axiality) or mechanically organized books (perhaps like Catullus' elegies?)[29] do not exploit the competent audience's initial expectations for a certain order, a certain

---

kind of commentary or canalizing of reception for the cycle of six poems the way a *lex arae* prescribes in pictorial or written form access to the implementation of an altar. For epigraphical evidence, cf. e.g., CIL VI, 826, III.1933, XII.4333. Horace's carefully composed *ordo legendi* constitutes a kind of canalizing as well, but the specific responses just mentioned in Books I, II and III function as a further particularization of the *ordo* into *lex,* to use Roman terms.

[27] The *Ara Pacis Augustae,* oriented East-West in antiquity, has been reconstructed on a North-South axis. The local topography, including the cremation area for Augustus and the imperial family, the Via and Porta Flaminia with its military implications, and other local features, combine into a rich context with unmistakable programmatic overtones for the altar itself. Torelli, *op. cit. supra,* n. 22, pp. 33-35, is instructive.

[28] See e.g., Frank E. Brown, *Roman Architecture* (New York, 1967), pp..30f.

[29] See W. V. Clausen, *op cit. supra* n. 23, pp. 40f.

marshalling of attention. After some degree of familiarity is generated, freedom to wander about on one's own, as it were, is a natural course.

The present investigation of strategems of placement creating context for the Roman Odes of Horace will now assume a state of awareness on the audience's part somewhat between the novelty of the text for a reader who has not "read through" the three books of *Odes*, and the comfortable familiarity the text exhibits for a reader who has experienced this corpus many times and controls almost total recall of it. We assume that the reader has read the corpus enough times to have an idea of what is where, but is by no means sure of the artistic reasons and effects of such an arrangement. This state of mind is probably a fair approximation for many post-antique readers of Horace and other ancient writers of poetry. It now remains to assess these artistic elements of the "frame" provided by the *ordo legendi* hitherto suggested.

The "frame" to be assumed for the six Roman Odes is made out of the hymn to Fortune and its antecedent personal experience of the divine, I.35 and 34 respectively, and III.24, a poem with no addressee and preoccupied with the corroding of Roman values chiefly through the misuse of wealth, and its pendant III.25, on Bacchic inspiration to compose something utterly new ("ad huc / indictum ore alio," lines 7f.) concerning Augustus' great work on earth and great reward in heaven. It should be repeated that each poem of this frame closest to the Roman Odes is twenty-three poems from that cycle's onset.

The poet presented in this grouping or frame undergoes a metamorphosis or development as startling as that presented in II.20, where he becomes a swan. In the beginning the persona of the poet characterizes himself as a skeptic concerning the divine, indeed, an adept in a system now seen as mad. In addition to the general interpretation of this system as Epicureanism,[30] the context created for I.34 by linking it to the poems under review here suggests also that Horace may be referring to his pessimism about the Roman state: a pessimism which the god's intervention on earth compels him temporarily at least to abandon. The *deus* here who controls the lightning and thunder that roars throughout the world and its depths is not much different from the *deus* of Odes III.1.5ff., though in the framing poem I.34 this god shades off into *Fortuna*, the subject of the great hymn I.35. This hymn advances views concerning the involvement of *Fortuna* with the stability of the state (I.35.13ff.), the safety of Augustus (29ff.) and the enterprises of the Eastern armies (29ff.) (thus dating the ode plausibly to 26 B.C.), and the morality of Rome's citizens

---

[30] Chester G. Starr, "Horace and Augustus," *American Journal of Philology* 90 (1969), p. 62, notes a movement away from Epicureanism to Stoicism in the later Horace.

(25ff.) who have indulged in civil war (33ff.), themes again to be found in the Roman Odes, and which the poet here presents in a pessimistic manner: "quid nos dura refugimus / aetas, quid intactum nefasti / liquimus?" (33ff.). To this must be compared III.6.45ff., where a very similar feeling of helplessness, of defeat pervades the close of the Roman Odes' cycle. But in between this first segment of the frame, where the poet turns his course away from his error of belief and toward concern about the state, and the Roman Odes themselves, he undergoes yet another change. He sees Bacchus, II.19, prophesies a new poetic utterance, II.20, pronounces it, III.1-6, and re-iterates its impact on the everyday life of his audience (though it seems probably true that III.24 was composed earlier it is nevertheless read "later") and arrogates to himself that status of being divinely inspired by Bacchus once more in III.25, re-authenticating the exalted source of the poems dealing with civic virtue, private morality, Caesar's exploits, and the stability of his rule. The poet Horace's own involvement with Augustus' goals can be charted from these six poems, I.34, 35, II.19, 20, III.24, 25, just as the citizen Horace's subsequent disenchantment can be assessed from other poetical works.[31] What is important to bear in mind is that Horace modulates his persona so that if we establish this particular concatenation of poems we can see him pass from being an error-ridden ignorer of the divine to one who not only acknowledges Fortune's sway over all the affairs of men and nations but even further is granted a personal vision of Bacchus teaching *carmina*, poems; he asserts forthcoming greatness for himself through art, utters the Roman Odes, and reiterates his deep concern for Rome as well as his Bacchic credentials. This ambitious program of increasing awareness and concomitant increasing poetic power is of course not so starkly visible if one reads all the intervening poems seriatim. But the identity of Alcaic meter for those singled out from Books I, II and III, and those meters recurring side by side, as well as the repetition of the second Asclepiadean in the sequence from the end of Book III, strongly suggest the validity of linking them to the Roman Odes as we have done. Finally, the equidistant frame, twenty-three poems on either side of III.1, suggests that no accidental or random placing should account for this collocation. The poet through ordering is manipulating our attention, and securing for the Roman Odes heightened qualities: they are objectified outside their own fabric and asserted to be *carmina* inspired by Bacchus, entirely novel, significant in a new way, securing their poet's immortality and linking the private and public worlds both of poet and of his audience through the medium of the Roman state.

---

[31] C. G. Starr, *op. cit. supra*, n. 30, pp. 62-64.

Without the state no Roman Odes, no immortality for Horace;[32] without
the state, no escape from the vortex of deliquescence, personal moral
decay, and resulting civic moral collapse for the individual citizen. The
Roman state, in the person of Caesar Augustus, is the bulwark between
error and oblivion rather than deathless universality for the poet, between deepening anomie, civic entropy and personal moral ruin rather
than purposeful existence for the citizen. The broad context for the
Roman Odes is both the poet and his audience, in a way more specially
created for these six poems than is usually the case. Poetic referrals to the
forthcoming cycle create a climate of considerable anticipation for them;
the subsequent validation of their message and their poet remind the
audience about to leave the lyric world of the *Odes* at the end of Book III
of the centrality of the Roman Odes, both for the corpus of texts, and for
the poet's artistic stature.

Perhaps some of the audience went even further, and heeded the moral
suasion of this complex aggregation of central monument, its prologue,
and its framing wings. Although the chief concern of the present study is
to present ways of competently reading the Roman Odes, nevertheless
this examination of their frame, rather like a study of the sculpture of the
Vestals and sacrificial animals on the wings of the *Ara Pacis Augustae*, its
lex arae, seeks to establish a general context for the leading features and
functions of the central monument itself.[33]

---

[32] Note the urban terms in which Horace at the end of the collection, III.30,
characterizes his monumentum (the Capitolium, vestal virgin, pontifex maximus.) See
also J. M. André, "Les Odes Romaines: Mission divine, otium et apothéose du chef,"
Hommages à Marcel Renard, ed. J. Bibauw, I (Paris, 1969), pp. 31-46.

[33] It might also be noted that Vergil, e.g. Georgic III.16ff., utilizes a mode of writing
that can be thought similar to the Roman historical relief, but without that development of
architectonic elements which can be seen in Horace. Further contrasts between the two
poets on this matter would perhaps be useful, and would probably suggest further basic
differences between Vergil's and Horace's conception of epic, as well as the problems of
Horace's combining epic and lyric and Vergil's combining in certain places epic and
pastoral; see M. C. J. Putnam, *Virgil's Poem of the Earth* (Princeton: Princeton University
Press, 1979), p. 168, "an architecture of mighty deeds."

CHAPTER THREE

THE FIRST ROMAN ODE

The competent reader of Horace's first Roman Ode may be relied upon to make certain observations and to establish certain connections as he re-reads this poem. Let us examine some of these as they occur in the ongoing process of reading this text.

The first four lines of the third book of *Odes* economically establish three operational categories: the speaker, the spoken and those spoken to (or not spoken to). Building on the exultation of II.20 and its authenticaton, II.19, the poet's self is revealed as occupying a privileged state: distinct from the non-initiates, and about to convey in the silence prescribed by ritual and demanded by his utterance of the formula "favete linguis," *carmina*, texts of great virtue and importance. It is the young to whom the poet speaks, those capable of implementing the vision which he mediates. A kind of ritual space is created by these four lines.[1] Its axis runs from the person of the *sacerdos* to those of the chosen audience, and the space excludes those not free enough from the yoke of time (their age, or the age itself) to heed the divinely qualified poet. No longer content as one of many to hymn the goddess Fortune of Anzio, the poet rises above the undifferentiated masses and appeals to a select audience: those who have acknowledged the supremacy of *Fortuna* go on to see in her a sign of God's greatest dimension: the ordering power of the divine. Spoken earlier but not heeded (*non audita*), these texts of high cultural, civic and religious import will create a new audience capable of heeding. Silence can betoken either negative qualities, silence resulting from its potential violators, the deniers, who are at a distance (*arceo*); or positive effects: silence maintained out of pious consent. (Originally Roman ritual called for silence in order to forestall any ill-omened words, a combination of these two functions.) It is up to the audience to choose one of these two rôles: to draw near in silence, or to withdraw in silence of another sort altogether.

The three verbs of this first strophe are in the first person singular; the poet who despises and repels also sings; it is the same person, this hierophant and poet; are the activities the same? That is, is the god-sent

---

[1] The use of "ritual space" in this connection is an extension of the idea of Frank E. Brown, *Roman Architecture* (New York, 1967), pp. 9-11. For Horace and religion, see R. Hanslik, "Die Religiosität des Horaz," *Altertum* I (1955), pp. 230-240, and T. Oksala, *Religion und Mythologie bei Horaz* (Helsinki, 1973).

vision and the god-inspired sacred text coterminous with estrangement from the undifferentiated *volgus* and its unprofound concerns? Possibly so. Sacred space must be cleared or defined for sacred acts; the setting up of the space, excluding as well as encapsulating, is indeed the first sacred action of a religious ritual. Within this *templum* the *profanum volgus* is hardly forgotten; rather, many references to it occur, as III.1 itself amply demonstrates. But it is the young, the pliable, those upon whom the performance of sacred text may make its deepest and longest-lasting effect, that are addressed in the enclosure of the Roman Odes. To forget this is to forget that one element of the cycle that gives it what unity it has. The poems with themes previously enunciated and not precisely heeded are here renewed; the poet, charged with the divine, turns his message into art (*musarum sacerdos*) and selects a special addressee for his messages.

He begins in a most unRoman way, by presenting, in line five, undifferentiated unRoman masses, *greges,* who are the property of very unRoman kings, *reges*: a departure from the status quo, a violation of audience expectation, inasmuch as it is a presentation of the world not from the viewpoint of the *greges* or of the *reges* but from Jupiter's: for him, kings and peoples are unspecified, unindividuated, the neuter plural *cuncta* of line eight. What lies behind this sweeping opening is the hymn to Zeus of Cleanthes, theologian of the early Stoa; [2] *ab Iove principium* is a very Roman way of expressing this idea of the dependency of all upon God, but it is usually presented from the perspective of the lower looking upward rather than the way Horace manages it here, from above, at a great distance (the after-effects of *arceo*) looking down on the great collectives of *reges* and their *greges*.

The principle of undifferentiation may even extend to the mention of the Giants in line seven; for it is usually the Titans, not the Giants, who are named in connection with Jupiter's great power, and to confuse them with the Giants may signal blurring or lack of identification because of disinterest and hence distance, like that associated with *odi* and *arceo,* line one.

The specificity of lines one through four, at least in regard to poet, audience and message, broken off by the sweeping generalizations of lines five through eight, may also suggest the prologue quality of verses one through four. However, lines nine following introduce a distillation of the particular, which obtains until *turba,* line thirteen, that undifferentiated *grex* of clients, which in turn leads back to the supernatural level and the

---

[2] Cf. also Callimachus' *Hymn to Zeus,* line 79. See as well V. Poschl, "Horaz," *L'Influence grecque sur la poésie latine de Catulle à Ovide, Entretiens sur l'antiquité* II, pp. 93-130, Fondation Hardt, (Genève, 1956).

force of *Necessitas*. If the *reges* have their *greges*, and Jupiter has both in sway, so too the individual has property, station, character, repute, and a following of clients, to greater or lesser degree in comparison with his fellows. As Jove rules rulers and peoples, so *Necessitas*, in that aspect of her akin to the *Fortuna* of I.35, and not as death,[3] is in control of high and low alike. Lines nine through sixteen repeat on the level of human affairs and from a more human perspective the points made in lines five through eight. However, Jupiter has become *Necessitas*, and the divine figure, far from perceiving undifferentiated masses of people, now knows your name: *cuncta*, the neuter plural, of line eight becomes *omne nomen* in line sixteen. This degree of particular awareness on the part of *Necessitas* is ominous, and may bode ill. Differentiation in degree of status on earth is levelled by the *aequa lex* of collectivization; the personal individualities represented by *est ut vir* are flattened by the gnomic quality of the utterance about the equal law. Property, ancestry, character, repute, political following, all the factors by which we distinguish social rôles and individuals, for *Necessitas* all are *nomen*.

If it be granted that *Necessitas* here is not death but adamantine fate sealing one's lot, then the impending terror of lines seventeen through twenty-four is terror of loss, of discovery: sleeplessness, worry, fears that dog the *cervix impia* do so not because of wealth only, but because they are tied to a particular station in life, for the *ensis* of line seventeen is quite clearly associated with not just any rich man, but with the tyrant of Sicily, Dionysius, whose dinner-guest, Damocles, sees the sword suspended over his host's head and draws conclusions about his vulnerability.[4] The rich tyrant is soon contrasted with men of low station, eking out a living in the country.

At the center of the poem a second gnomic utterance occurs: *desiderantem quod satis est*, line twenty-five; this person, in contrast to *cui* of line seventeen, is not evidently a merchant dependent on the weather signs for late sailings, about to be mentioned, nor a farmer, who is

---

[3] It is often assumed that *Necessitas* in III.1.14 is Death, e.g., Gordon Williams, *The Third Book of Horace's Odes* (Oxford: Oxford University Press, 1969), *ad. loc.* and p. 125. However, the work of E. T. Silk has convincingly shown that this need not be the case: "Towards a Fresh Interpretation of Horace Carm. III.1," *Yale Classical Studies* 23 (1973), pp. 139-145. On III.1, see also Eduard Fraenkel, *Horace* (Oxford: Oxford University Press, 1957), pp. 261ff., and Steele Commager, *The Odes of Horace* (New Haven: Yale University Press, 1962), p. 16, and V. Pöschl, "Die Einheit der ersten Römerode," *Harvard Studies in Classical Philology* 63 (1958), pp. 333-346, and especially his *Horazische Lyrik: Interpretationen* (Heidelberg, 1970), pp. 144-164, the only Roman Ode treated in this valuable book. See also E. T. Silk, "The God and the Searchers for Happiness: Notes on Horace's Repetition and Variation of a favorite *Topos,*" *Yale Classical Studies* 19 (1966), pp. 241-244 on III.1 (and I.35 and III.3 in contrast).

[4] G. Williams, *op. cit. supra*, n. 3, *ad loc.* gives the argument.

likewise dependent. In fact it is impossible, in the terms provided by the
text, to assign the man who desires what is enough any specific rôle or
station. By implication he, like the *viri agrestes* of lines twenty-two
following, through contrast with the *impia cervix* of line seventeen, is *pius*,
and obviously *desiderat quod satis est*. But if he were a small farmer, one
with a *humilis domus*, line twenty-two, he would be ruined by such
weather as is described in lines twenty-nine following. Clearly Horace
has shifted to the problem of attitude, away from the problem of social
categories. Otherwise, if one were to regard the *viri agrestes* as still in the
network of communication, as it were, after the gnomic *desiderantem quod
satis est*, one would be compelled to judge Horace inconsistent,
unrealistic, and even unfair to farmers. Commentators, by characterizing the recipient of the bad weather as a great property owner, do but
read into the text a solution to a problem they do not read out of the text.[5]
A small farm suffers total loss, their reasoning may be supposed to run,
so the poet must be concerning himself with a large farmer greedy for
more than his due. But obviously the point is made in regard to *quod satis
est* as the object of desire. Attitude is superordinate here just as in
preceding strophes; one has to be aware of the hanging sword, or of the
troubles it symbolizes, before being so worried as to be insomniac.
Farmers know no sword, and work hard too, and therefore sleep: so
would run the logic of the "real" world if imported to the poem. But the
poet is not dealing with psychological commonplaces or truisms, but with
a special vision of the world and himself in it. Those who work for subsistence, for maintenance, for *quod satis est*, sleep; those who want more
do not rest easily; and over all is the *imperium* of heaven, containing all is
the vessel of fate. Awareness of the sword, or sound sleep or its absence,
are meaningless distinctions in a world where natural process is so altered
as to admit trees that put blame for low yield on flood, drought, and cold,
and fish that feel constrained by marine architectural ventures (lines thirty following).[6] Rather, it is the striving for elaboration (line nineteen,
elaborabunt; cf. *moliar*, line forty-six), the crossing of natural barriers sym-
bolized by building over and in water[7] that is held up for question. The
farmer is no more aware of *Necessitas* or the god than is the rich man;

---

[5] This is the approach of standard commentators, e.g., *Q. Horatius Flaccus Oden und
Epoden*[9] ed. Adolf Kiessling and Richard Heinze (Berlin, 1958), *ad loc.*, hereafter referred
to as Kiessling-Heinze.

[6] This is not the hyperbole that Kiessling-Heinze, *ad loc.*, assert.

[7] Building programs over the water at Anzio were carried out; the most renowned were
those of Nero, revealed in Allied bombardment of Anzio during World War II. Cf. also J.
E. G. Whitehorne, "The Ambitious Builder," *Journal of the Australasian Universities
Language and Literature Association* 31 (1969), pp. 28-39, and L. Alfonsi, "Notes de lecture,"
Latomus 20 (1961), pp. 845-846 on III.1. 33f.

perhaps even less so. He is merely free of worry because he has less to lose: only *quod satis est.* He does not work harder than is needed to achieve *qoud satis est:* but by whose criterion? Surely in the end, in the *capax urna,* it does not matter.

Those who, like Gordon Williams,[8] try to make this poem into a connected discursive statement are obliged to treat it roughly. The poem rather exhibits various layers susceptible to various interpretations and an endless range of significance, as has just been demonstrated. To confine observation solely to interpretations: Williams avers that "the thought in the poet's mind, was basically: 'What is the point of personal ambition?'"[9] and relates this to wealth on the one hand, and quiet country living on the other. It apparently occasions no surprise that a text prepared for so lavishly and sacrally as III.1 can be reduced to "Live an unambitious life." Yet if one remains shackled to the literal, to the discursive, to the text isolated from its context of other poems in the cycle, this is the kind of interpretation that must result. The fault lies not in the logic of such a superb critic as Williams but in not having a critical method that does more than examine "the relationship of the great generalization" (5-8) to the rest," which is this critic's diagnosis of "the problem in this poem."[10] Poems need not be or exhibit problems. The reader is always the problem, usually because he is reading the text in the wrong context, or sometimes the wrong text. Here enough has been said about the solemn preparation for III.1 to show that it is very likely not simply an enunciation of a basic moral which "function[s] simply as an underlying principle."[11] Williams is right when he draws attention to the unpredictable contrasting pictures presented in the sweep of III.1, and he does well to stress their dominant quality. But it is these "pictures" alone that constitute the text, not any underlying moral which may well be a cultural pre-text, or a post-textual extrapolation, and as such should be carefully demarcated from the text by any responsible critical operation. Let us turn to a somewhat detailed examination of the text itself in hopes of recovering grounds for an interpretation on the text's own terms.

I have above suggested that the poem forms halves. The first half has the *viri agrestes* (plural) for a foil to the *impia cervix* (singular) of the very singular tyrant of Sicily; a gentle breeze refreshes these humble country dwellers. In the second half a similar armature can easily be discerned:

---

[8] G. Williams, *op. cit. supra,* n. 3, *ad loc.* See also Hendrik Wagenvoort, *De Horatii quae dicuntur Odis Romanis* (Groningen, 1911), pp. 18-47 (on III.1 and 2). This work is also useful on all the Roman Odes.

[9] G. Williams, *ibid.,* and p. 32.

[10] G. Williams, *ibid.*

[11] G. Williams, *ibid.*

the *pisces* (plural) form a foil for the excesses of the *redemptor / dominus* (singular) whom a violent desire to alter the natural landscape assails. Other elements that suggest a mirroring effect in the two reaches of the poem include a sound pattern *desiderantem quod satis est* (25) and *quodsi dolentem* (41) in the first and second halves respectively. Further, note how *desiderantem quod satis est* is followed by the connectives *neque, nec, aut* (25ff.); its phonic kin, *quodsi dolentem*, is followed by *nec, nec, nec* (41ff.), the densest array of connectives in the poem. The two passages reinforce each other; the man who desires what is enough and the sick man are closely parallel (if not identical). The text seeks to level syntactically and phonically the very distinctions it lexically and semantically advances.

Further evidence of similarities between the beginning and end of this message can easily be found. The first person singular occurs only in the first and last strophes. Future passive participles occur only in line five (*timendorum regum*) and line forty-five (*invidendis postibus*). In contrast, personifications are confined to a central area, *fundus mendax* (30), *Timor, Minae* (37), *Cura* (40). Perfect passive participles abound everywhere, e.g., 3, 17, 24, 29, 33, 34, 39. Present active participles in the genitive are (*Iovis*) *moventis*, 8, (*Arcturi*) *cadentis*, 27, and (*Haedi*) *orientis*, 28, all celestial, a suggestive array. Lexically, (*non*) *fastidit*, 23, and the prominently placed *fastidiosus*, 37, are the mainsprings of the poem. Sleep does not scorn humble lodgings (but does evade the worried tyrant); the rich man disdains the land (but not the wrong element, the water) yet worry catches up with him at sea or on land. The man who is *fastidiosus* is not *impius* (nor does he explicit undergo the experience of the *impius* in this poem) but neither does he desire *quod satis est*. There is land enough for man, but he goes to build on the alien sea. Yet in the world of this poem, if there be any consistency the land is also *mendax*[12] when it comes to providing man with sustenance.

A pattern of equivalency, latent in these examples, may now be set forth. Poem III.1, the first Roman Ode, is a declarative poem; there is no subjunctive in it except for the *est ut* construction, 9ff. (Contrast should be made by the reader later with III.2 and its initial jussive subjunctives, III.2.3ff.) This poem establishes a context, a world, makes distinctions, and orders its reality. It uses the interrogative form only twice, both in the last strophe: the two questions contain in their formulation two words that provide their answers: *sublime* and *operosiores*. Aspirations are sure to elicit hostile reactions from others; the city brings worries along with riches; why change? But what one should bear in mind is that the poet is left not in respectable rural shabbiness but clothed with the importance of

---

[12] Note the context of *mendax* here, and cf. Petronius, *Satyricon* 117.

the first strophe. His Sabine valley is the retreat of the Muses, a setting for his art, not merely for his humble historical social self. The poet is not engaged in differentiating two selves in the first and last strophes of this poem any more than he is distinguishing between kings that must be feared and despots sure to be envied: both are operations resulting from the perspective of the world from which the poet is seeking to free others, as he himself has been freed by the authenticating vision he proclaims. The *aequa lex Necessitatis* brings all to one end; things cannot help the human condition, be it *desiderans* or *dolens*; they are much the same, for even if one is *desiderans quod satis est,* the same awaits. God rules, kings reign, and man is either ill at ease or at home in the world; but the world's things, beyond mere subsistence, are useless in making a difference to man. Much depends on rulers and on heaven; but even with benevolent rule and good weather, the same end awaits.

Those who see the Roman Odes ending, with III.6, in an unforeseen pessimism should bear in mind that III.1 is not exactly optimistic in tone, but rather is solemnly dark and resignedly passive in the face of *Necessitas,* Jupiter and, in the background *Fortuna* herself. Far from issuing didactic calls to take attitudes or actions, the poet here advances brilliant pictures of the futility of personal drive, personal power, personal possessions. The next ode will introduce a new term in this lexicon of possibilities: the state.

Several elements common to the Roman Odes as a whole are introduced in III.1. Among these are the interplay of abstract personifications such as *Necessitas, Timor, Minae, Cura,* and vivid concrete details, such as *Siculae dapes, Phrygius lapis,* etc. Further, the incipient tension between the personal rôle or aspect of the poet as contrasted with his public side might also be raised as a question. In the terms of III.1, is the *vallis Sabina* not only the stronghold of art, as here suggested, but also that comfortable fastness of private cultivation, and are *divitiae operosiores* public and civic pronouncements and responsibilities? In the dynamics of III.1, the question can be asked but not answered. Further interpretation of the Roman Odes may, however, suggest an avenue for approaching this question.

If the poet's outburst about *quod si dolentem* (41f) is made up of sounds similar to *desiderantum quod satis est* (25) and if an assimilation of even the non-ambitious to the sick at heart—sick with the illness of human existence—can be made, so too parallelism or assimilation can be seen elsewhere knitting the text into a comprehensive assertion of this vision of the world. First, both Roman examples (strophes 3 and 4, and 7ff) and non-Roman examples (strophes 2 and 5) show the universality of this poet's visionary scope. Next, one may observe how the text passes from vast concerns (eastern kings and their peoples) to the Roman merchant and farmer, thus preparing the way for the poet to re-appear in civic guise at the end. He is the same poet as in strophe 1, but functions as *cives* and not as *vates*. Finally, the superordinate rule of Jupiter and the underlying control of *Necessitas* are transformed into a sword suspended over a neck, and the weather (about which indeed nothing can be done) becomes a local manifestation of *Necessitas*. The grand and universal continually shade into the particular and the everyday, but of course not presented in everyday language or tone. The personifications of 37ff. do much to elevate the tone, and to show that it is to the powerful and prominent man that the poet wishes to draw final attention before breaking off his pictures of cosmic ruler and leveller contrasted with their mundane means of operation.[13]

Far from being a text enjoining contentment with one's lot and discouraging personal ambition, the first Roman Ode is a psychological model of a social state: God's control, capable of being articulated on a grand scale, shades off into the everyday where it is no longer perceived except in social terms: *quod satis est, dominus terrae fastidiosus,* etc. Yet the outriders of divine permeation of the world's fabric, *Timor, Minae, Cura,* objectify the interior state of the man who is *dolens,* in spite of his success, wealth and power, economic and hence social. Artistic retreat breaks their power and suffuses it with the right perspective: all is in the sway of God, *Necessitas* knows all our names.

Perhaps Friedrich Solmsen was right for a reason he did not advance when he observed[14] that *Odes* III.1 may urge young Romans to seek individual happiness, rather than to help build up the new Rome of Augustus. When all levels, social, economic and political, are illusions before the great power of God and the levelling law of *Necessitas,* one must realize the futility of aspirations that well up from individual or collective man. A higher power must support, strengthen and validate any such efforts; having dismantled, in III.1, the world bereft of this direct intervention of heaven and its concomitant social organ, the state, and having shown its vanity, the poet goes on in III.2 to show a rudimentary evolution of civic awareness built upon the absolute zero, the chilling denials and hard realities of III.1.

This theory of reading applied to III.1 obliges us to postulate as well a theory of taste, an interpretation or set of interpretations (one of many

---

[13] A word about *Timor, Minae* and the armor-plated trireme may be useful. Almost all commentators, ancient, medieval, Renaissance and modern, suggest the context of civilian life. However, the presence of *Timor* and *Minae,* twin companions of Mars (like *Phobos* and *Deimos* of Ares) suggest that a warlike setting is not to be ruled out. If so, there is a slight anticipation here of the subsequent ode's preoccupation at its outset with war.

[14] Friedrich Solmsen, "Horace's First Roman Ode," *American Journal of Philology* 68 (1943), p. 338.

possibilities) for the text just discussed. We have moved from the phenomenology of the writer's consciousness to our framework of understanding, but not without a suspicion that Horace's poem (here as well as elsewhere in his corpus) resists the, or even a, final meaning, and goes on proliferating interpretations endlessly: no unusual result for a text as shifting, dynamic and vivid as III.1 can easily be discerned to be.

CHAPTER FOUR

THE SECOND ROMAN ODE

If *Odes* III.1 sets at naught the vivid riches of the East and of Italy herself in face of their inability to alter the inner state of *homo dolens,* and consequently calls into question the reasonableness of all striving in the areas of agriculture, commerce, civic life, and even personal character, in light of *Necessitas* and her *aequa lex,* the second movement of the Roman Odes takes its inception from what is left of social life in the world: very little indeed, *angusta pauperies* of the poem's first line. But before examining III.2 in light of its predecessor—and this light is crucial for a deeper awareness of the function of III.2—let us examine this text first as a relatively independent entity.[1]

Formal observations may be a quick way of setting up categories which suggest ways of approaching this text. We note that the first three strophes are not end-stopped, and that the next three strophes are end-stopped; finally, the last but one is not end-stopped. Thus the text can be broken into three parts on these grounds, viz., Strophes 1-3, 4-6 and 7-8.

The subjunctives or optatives *condiscat, vexet, agat, suspiret,* and *lacessat* all occur in the first three strophes; the only other subjunctive in the poem is *sit,* line twenty-eight, taking *volgarit* as future perfect, and the only indicative in the first three strophes is *rapit,* line twelve. Hence one may observe that III.2.1-2 is the opposite in choice of verbal mood from III.1, where the indicative prevailed. The first three strophes at least of III.2 are no description of an everyday world, but a set of injunctions to the Roman boy of Augustus' day: grown hard through military service, let him learn to bear constraining poverty as a friend; let him go on foreign campaigns and experience exotic encounters; and so forth. It may be noted that each of these injunctions to the Roman youth is for the benefit of a group rather than for the self; does the avenue of escape from being *homo dolens* lie perhaps in service to others? References to the *lusus Troiae,* and to Augustus' preoccupations with the revival of the *collegia iuvenum* may be apposite here.[2] But the inner dynamic rather than the outward organizational forms is that to which the poet seeks to draw attention.

---

[1] For a different but fruitful approach see P. J. Connor, "The Balance Sheet: Considerations of the Second Roman Ode," *Hermes* 100 (1972), 241-248; also Steele Commager, *The Odes of Horace* (New Haven: Yale University Press, 1962), pp. 13ff., 21f., 105, 308. See as well E. Cameron, "An Analysis of Horace, Odes III.2," *Akroterion* 18 (1973), pp. 17-22.

[2] So Kiessling-Heinze *ad loc.*

It has not hitherto been noticed, I believe, that the first three strophes exhibit, in lexical choice, the crossing of two themes prominent in Roman poetry of Augustus' day: the erotic (not found in civic poetry) and the military.[3] Should a critic of Roman literature be told of a twelve-line Alcaic Augustan text, now lost or in fragments, containing the words *amice, pati, militia, puer, sub divo, vitam trepidis, matrona, adulta virgo, suspiret, eheu, sponsus, lacessat, tactu* and *ira,* he could with a certain degree of confidence say he was dealing with an erotic message. If he were told that his text exhibited the words *angustam pauperiem, robustus acri militia, Parthos ferocis, vexet eques, metuendus hasta, moenibus hosticis, bellantis tyranni, asperum leonem, cruenta* and *caedes,* he would opine that the text was of an entirely different order: historical or civic poetry (or a *recusatio* of such a theme). What is interesting is that the reader of III.2 is not usually aware of the large element of words dealing with erotic subject matter in the first twelve lines because of their context: especially because of the memorable *sententia* of line thirteen. This is precisely Horace's strategem: the "love interest" of life is subordinate to, and hence forgotten (but only temporarily; see III.7!) in the context of non-selfish expenditure of energy, specifically military service to the state.

The poem is a model of what it inculcates. Not in some ways unlike a modern military recruitment poster, with its allurements of exotica if not erotica, the opening stage of III.2 puts into the background, and hence into circulation in the text, the theme of personal love, only to subordinate it to the overriding concerns of personal hardihood and strength in the context of poverty; *amice* can thus be seen as the word pivoting between the erotic world and the world of renunciation of personal entanglement and ambition.[4]

The tension between the two worlds of peace and war, personal pursuits and collectivized action, is worked out not in a Roman context, but in the scene[5] of the second and third strophes wherein the mother and her daughter are caught up in gazing at the Roman youth (one of a horde, one must fancy, but particularized because of the amatory context) and in concern about his bringing woe to their own man. Their female, foreign perspective is turned toward the personal, on individuals, like

---

[3] Ovid was not the first to link military and erotic metaphor, e.g., his "militat omnis amans," *Amores* I.9.1. The image goes back much farther, e.g., Sappho, fragments 1,16, 31. See now the dissertation of Leah Rissman, "Homeric Allusion in the Poetry of Sappho," The University of Michigan, 1980, pp. 54-102, for a complete discussion.

[4] Late antique commentators and mediaeval scribes take *amice* as the vocative of *amicus,* and thus title III.2 "Ad amicos," etc. Was Horace's strategem too clever to be picked up even by an antique audience?

[5] The scene is reminiscent of *Iliad* III.146-60, where the rôles are reversed: Helen is watched by old men from the walls of Troy.

scenes from a civic monument. Their viewpoint is whirled away through
the reflection by the poet (13ff.) on the slaughter they are witnessing: the
famous line "dulce et decorum est pro patria mori."[6]

These three opening run-on strophes present two worlds in collision:
the poor Roman youth, the rich foreign tyrant; Rome facing her enemy.
It is through self-denial, the *pauperies* of line one, that the *puer* takes
ascendancy over the *tyrannus*: the same cast of characters as Dionysius
and the farmers in III.1, but in the setting of Rome at war. This element
in the moral calculus of values encountered hitherto in the Roman Odes
is a new one, an advance over the values purveyed in III.1, wherein the
viri agrestes remained in their setting, as it were, and were not
transplanted for the common good; their *pauperies* was economic. In the
very first line of III.2 it is energized, linked to a higher cause, and
assigned a function. Likewise the rich persons in III.1 are revealed with a
new aspect in III.2: they become the *regius sponsus*, the foreign enemy all
too close to Paris in the *Iliad*, that type for Antony, for Rome's own
comfort.

Out of this collision of rich and poor, private and public, amatory and
military, come three end-stopped strophes. Lines 13-16 speak of war and
death in such a way that the enhacement secured by a death for the *patria*
is somewhat undercut by the poet's subsequent remark that death comes
after even the fleeing man. As Gordon Williams tells us, in some situations a man's life is inevitably to be lost, and he might as well exploit this
situation rather than die a coward.[7] This is of course true (though one
could debate whether men in such situations reason so), but we must take
stock of the fact that this is an importation of "real world" logic into a
literary artifice. In terms of the world of the Roman Odes, one might
assert that the *Necessitas* of III.1.14[8] has become *Mors* here, and that the
aequa lex still prevails; though the context is ostensibly the battlefield (*pro
patria mori* has this strong implication), still the *et* of line fourteen, and the
virtual oxymoron of *vir fugax* (ibid.), the indeterminate age of the youth of
unwarlike disposition, and the back that seeks to shun pursuing death, all
conspire to suggest a transitional context as well. Death gets everyone,
omne nomen III.1.16). There is no need to see in this fourth strophe only a
battlefield scene, though war is I believe uppermost in the layers of
possible interpretations.

The *Necessitas* of III.1 prevails also in the world of III.2, wherein
pauperies, a private condition, gives way to military endeavor abroad

---

[6] See H. Hommel, "Dulce et decorum," *Rheinisches Museum* 111 (1968), pp. 219-252.
[7] G. Williams, *The Third Book of Horace's Odes* (Oxford: Oxford University Press, 1969),
p. 35.
[8] See n. 3, p. 21 *supra*.

(public work), a romanticized encounter and finally death made significant (*dulce* from the erotic or private world-view; *decorum* from the self-abnegating viewpoint of the state), because it is *pro patria*. The *vir fugax* of line fourteen may be thought of as fleeing more than death; poverty can also be fled, but one winds up dead anyway; the poet thus recaptures III.1.37f. in this crossing of themes to make an incremental structure we call the Roman Odes. Poverty, both the economic condition and the narrowness of spirit, is what is left behind by the Roman youth in service to his country; it is what the selfish man, even if rich, cannot escape. Both indeed obey an *aequa lex*; but the one, though *pauper*, attains *decus* and *dulcitia*; the other, though rich, has only death as an end to his spiritual and civic poverty of life. War has made the *puer* of III.2.2 the equal battle antagonist of a royal prince; this is but another aspect of the levelling law, *lex aequa*, of *Necessitas*. War ideally if not in actuality makes prince and peasant equal when they are also in service to the state on the same fighting side, one may presume: or at least their deaths in the cause of the state should be equally deserving of recognition and the epithets *dulce* and *decorum*. Thus the equality of all in death can be asserted in III.2 in a more positive way than in III.1.

Strophes five through eight, the rest of III.2, turn from the private or individualized sphere, with their coloring of romanticism, to the public sphere, specifically to the public man's commitment to public good. Thus strophe four can be seen to be pivotal in another way: its retrospective elements include *dulce, iuventa,* etc., the romantic side of strophes 1-3, and its prospective elements (for the reader who has read all the text, *a fortiori* all the Roman Odes) include *patria* and the *vir*; the negative *virum fugacem* becomes transformed into the positive *virtus*, lines seventeen and twenty-one.

If III.1 dealt with *quod satis est*, the even keel of balance, of moderation, III.2 begins with *pauperies*, a point a good deal lower than *quod satis est*, and soars to the level of *virtus* once the *pauperies* is put into a social context free of personal concern. Thus liberated, as it were, through consideration of war, the poet can concern himself with *virtus* in peace, which characteristic emerges through the dramatic rise of the Roman youth through civic service. The private *puer*, socialized by military service, may, in another aspect, generate benefit for the community through civil responsibilities; his qualities of being a man, *vir*, result also in this kind of *virtus*. In line seventeen, *repulsae* (used only here in all of Horace's lyrics) looks as much back to the military sphere and to the inability of death to shock *virtus*, as it does forward to the civic sphere, wherein *virtus* does not register setbacks or react to popular whim. It is the genius of Horace to use such pivot words with the effects here briefly noted by the attentive reader reading cumulatively. The principal context for *repulsa,* whereby its significance of defeat is conferred, is the soliciting of public office. Yet it is not until *honoribus* (line eighteen) and *securis* (line nineteen) are reached that this context is securely established. Until then, *repulsa* can and does have military overtones. *Virtus* (now in its new civilian context) is negatively characterized as not acknowledging disgrace in defeat: a brief glance, perhaps, toward the "real" world wherein Augustus in 28 B.C. embarked on social reforms, the laws for which were rejected by the Senate.[9] The failure did not cause his regime to confess defeat, however. So too here, *virtus* is not diminished in its honors, and does not put much store in public whim. This stance is a familiar one for the poet to take, as at *Odes* III.1.1ff.; we shall return to this point later.

If in strophe five *virtus* is characterized by contrast with defeat and honors that are corroded or dulled (just as the *puer* of the first strophe is characterized by contrast with the regal *sponsus*) so in the sixth strophe *virtus,* again prominently named (or is it named again to signal a shift in its meaning?) is characterized by distinction once again from the *volgus* (cf. III.1.1; *coetus volgaris*) and the damp earth, and by its property of opening heaven to those deserving of immortality.[10]

One should note how the positive injunctions of the first three strophes relying on the subjunctive and in run-on form are succeeded by end-stopped strophes that use the indicative to set forth certain characteristics by negative contrasts. The process begins technically with line fifteen, *nec,* and continues with *nescia,* line seventeen, *intaminatis,* line eighteen, *nec-aut,* line nineteen, *inmeritis,* line twenty-one, *negata,* line twenty-two, and, if not lexically at least semantically, *fugiente,* line twenty-four. We are now in a position to recognize *virtus* by what it does not do: an accurate measure for the policy of Augustus around 28 B.C., and one rarely met with in government before or since. The concrete particularization of strophes 1-3, even with their romantic tone, give way to three strophes of abstraction; the alteration, though not so tidily symmetrical, was noted above for III.1.[11]

But the poet goes on to concrete examples again, which, like other elements in the poem, are perhaps unexpected by the reader involved with understanding or even anticipating this poem's subtleties[12] but

---

[9] E.g., Suetonius, *Augustus* 34.

[10] On virtue opening the gate of heaven, see Simonides fr. 99 Bgk, 121D and G. J. Sullivan, "Horace, Odes III.2.21," *Classical Journal* 58 (1963), pp. 267f.

[11] See pp. 20f. *supra.*

[12] G. Williams, *op. cit. supra,* n. 7, p. 34: a "surprising idea"; p. 35: a "surprising view... a curious scene... curiously unpoetical realism"; p. 36: "an unexpected turn, ... a puzzling poem."

which can easily be demonstrated to be at home in a certain context, generating and canalizing certain interpretations. These last two strophes are, like the opening ones, not end-stopped, but unlike them, they contain four, not two, sentences. Four classes or entities are contrasted: faithful silence and its reward; the faithful person and the betrayer, the former being easily assimilatable into the poet's persona; the guiltless and the guilty: *Poena* (a kind of reward) and the criminal. Again binary opposites combine to produce the general picture. The setting is not war, but ostensibly private life, wherein initiations, visits and travel go forward in a setting of house-beams and yachts: no *pauperies* here. Yet all these activities are monitored by heaven: a factor not met with in this ode, except in the rather general *caelum*, line twenty-two, here the goal of those undeserving of death and not an entity watching man and his doings. Yet we have seen the Roman youth *sub divo*, line five, and this specification for his basic training is to be linked to the old form *Diespiter*, Sky-father, line twenty-nine; the *puer* (after the poem is finished) may be thought to have enjoyed some divine attention after all, and even be among those enjoying the apotheosis of the sixth strophe. *Pauperies* had its reward; does its opposite not have its dangers? It is the moneyed who might more often be in a position to betray a confidence, a religious (or political) mystery's arcana, to board a yacht after not paying proper tendance to Diespiter, and to get a fair head-start on Vengeance.

Rome and her external enemies were in collision in strophes 1-4; her internal enemies form the foils for the positive values purveyed in the rest of the poem. Both sets of observations are framed by the poet whose pastoral self at the end of III.1 does not (or should not) eclipse the poet of power, enjoining silence at the outset of III.1. This may be the moment to raise the question of what the *merces* may be for the faithful silence of III.2.24f. Note that the context is one with strong affinities to the first Roman Ode. *Est et* (III.2.25) is parallel to *est ut* (III.1.9): the poet in declarative mood; further, the silence of III.1.1ff. is of religious dimensions, and in III.2.26 the religious context retrospectively colors the *silentium fidele* of the preceding line. We have had occasion elsewhere to examine Horace's connection of divine inspiration, the poet's exalted status and his poetic productions; it may not be amiss to assess the whole of III.2 in this light.[13]

---

[13] See D. O. Ross, Jr., *Backgrounds to Augustan Poetry* (Cambridge: Cambridge University Press, 1975), pp. 141-152, for Horace's artistic views as related to Calllimachus, Vergil and putatively Gallus. Such assertions are obviously programmatic; see also W. Wimmel, *Kallimachos in Rom*, *Hermes Einzelschrift* 16 (Wiesbaden, 1960), and L. Lindo, "Tyrtaeus and Horace Odes III.2," *Classical Philology* 66 (1971), pp. 258ff.; also N. B. Crowther, "Horace, Catullus and Alexandrianism," *Mnemosyne* 31 (1978), pp. 33-44.

The *merces* of III.2.26 must proceed from either the gods or their representative. Elsewhere Horace has unambiguously called attention to this function of poetry: *Odes* IV.9, addressed to Lollius and obviously composed after the first three books of *Odes,* can be seen as a kind of gloss on certain aspects of III.2, and suggests that the *merces* may be in the form of poetic signalization of the deserving party. The ode in question exhibits certain similarities to III.2. We may begin by observing its meter, the Alcaic, and collocation of *pauperiem pati,* IV.9.49 and III.2.1, both at the same place in the line, both at the beginning of a strophe, the last one of IV.9, the first one of III.2. *Pati* located at the end of a line is also to be seen in III.24.42 in connection with *pauperies,* one of the "frames" of the Roman Odes, and in I.1.18. The context of each bears scrutiny. The collocation seems a favorite of Horace, but this does not deprive it of programmatic significance. Next, the occurrence of *silebo* (IV.9.30) and *fidus* IV.9.40) may also be a weak parallel to *fideli silentio* (III.2.25). But more to the point, the poet who in IV.9 spends a good deal of time involved with the subject of his art also in III.1 and III.2 may easily be discerned at the same activity. In III.1, the ceremonial beginning and more modest conclusion need no further comment in this connection. In III.2, the poet emerges toward the end in the word *vetabo,* line twenty-six, the only first-person verb in the whole text. But is he absent from the rest of the poem? Hardly; it is his perspective that encompasses the injunctions and assertions in all preceding strophes, and the subsequent concluding one as well. In that case, can one say that the *virtus* twice mentioned (17, 21) may exhibit a facet in addition to the ones hitherto suggested? If it be related to art, specifically to the poet's craft in its civic context, interesting movements occur in III.2 and in relation to III.1 (and IV.9) as well. Let us conjecture that the first three strophes of III.2, signalized as a unit by their run-on character (two sentences in three strophes), the *puer* and his audience, a very "poetical" as well as political subject, may be seen as furnishing a subject for poetry, indeed, for the poetic process engaging the reader of III.2.1ff. If the end of III.1 presents the poet in pastoral retreat, III.2 shows him as a civic poet. It is poetry that can and does objectify the memorable assertion "dulce et decorum est pro patria mori," (13) and thus confers what the adjectives betoken. It is poetry, a special kind of *virtus,* that soars, is independent, shuns the damp earth and common herd, and (the point of IV.9) confers immortality on certain men. Poetry also does not say all it knows to say: "est et fideli tuta silentio / merces..." (25f.). And that *merces* is linked to the civic rôle assumed by the poet or assigned him by Bacchus or the state itself. When God is *neglectus,* when there is no proper tendance, no proper cult, one can assume (along with III.6.1ff.) that the *merces* is withheld. One thinks of

III.2.26 *merces* and III.3.22ff., where the gods are defrauded *mercede pacta*; surely a case of loss of faith and gross neglect of the gods. Though tl.e poet (and others too) be *integer* (cf. I.22.1) and lead a life of quiet reclusion (the end of III.1) he can still be swept along with the guilty into death: the *lex aequa* of III.1.14 seen from a new and disturbing viewpoint.

Death overtakes all, to be sure: but poetry can and does call attention to those dying bravely (like Regulus, III.5) and makes their action *dulce et decorum*. Poetry is what ennobles, for it makes available the nobility of those who distinguish themselves by dying or living in special ways. Horace invents the word *intaminatis*, III.2.18, occurring only here in earlier Latin; his poetic act forges both the word and the thing it describes, and he draws unmistakable attention through the fabric of his language and of this linguistic coinage to the innovating power of this *virtus* of art.

At the outset of his monumental cycle, the poet has announced *carmina non prius audita,* poems not previously heeded or heard, or, in other words, those containing advice or warning not previously heeded; he thereby implies or even invites examination of the process of transmitting the advice or warning; that is, he makes the monument assert its objective existence as a monument (just as plastic works of art do), and so involves the text and its reader in a presentation of the poetic self and in questions concerning the function and status or mode of existence of his kind of civic poetry. Poetry is central to the passage *est ut,* III.1, strophe three, and *est et,* III.2, strophe seven. The poet in III.1 also desires *quod satis est*; hence his credentials. The poet is in accord with nature, and may be implementing a stoic view of willing one's fate. With this established, the poet speaks III.2, presenting a picture, strophes 1-3, and a reaction to it, strophes 4-6, which becomes *his* reaction, strophes 7-8, with the only first-person singular verb of the poem, line twenty-six. As *integer* and *intaminatus,* the *vates* is like the self-by-contrast he exhibited in III.1, in which luxury characterizes a negative way of life, whereas in III.2 poverty characterizes the positive way of the poem, of a subject for literature.

If a natural world order is set forth in III.1 with its priamel of *est ut,* the means for transcending such an order is shown by III.2 which characterizes *virtus* as getting beyond the "givens" of the natural world (*negata via,* line twenty-two). A via media, *desiderans quod satis est,* in the material world is purveyed by III.1; there is no middle or prudent way in III.2, wherein death comes to the brave and the coward alike. The style of one's life is what matters here: and it is a style of life not characterized by *quod satis est* but by going beyond this, subsuming *virtus* and storming heaven itself. It is as if Horace has in the first two Roman Odes set up equations of which he leaves one part unstated. In III.1 life is the setting;

luxury implies a negative valuation; *quod satis est* implies the poet's positive self, his social rôle. But in III.2, art and the state are the setting; poverty implies a positive valuation; and, what Horace does not state, viz., going beyond *quod satis est* in a special context, civic and spiritual service, implies what the ode dwells on in its second and final phase, *virtus*, a subject for art as for the state.

The self of the poet is prominent in both closures of both poems. In III.1 he has established his social identity; in III.2 he presents what his art can do in the nature of celebrating *virtus,* and in the nature of silence; a powerful medium, his art cannot say all it sees or knows, or the state or the art might be harmed in some unspecified way. The silence of uncomplaining poverty is akin to the silence of a rich mind: *merces* exists for both. At the end of III.3, and throughout much of III.4, the poet is likewise in the foreground of his text, mediating his vision of Rome's destiny and its divine qualifications, and of the shaping force of its art. He has carefully prepared his audience's frame of reference for this more ambitious picture of himself through III.1 and III.2.

CHAPTER FIVE

THE THIRD ROMAN ODE

Although manuscript evidence suggests that it was by no means anomalous to reproduce the whole cycle of Roman Odes as one long poem,[1] it is obvious on intrinsic evidence that the texts are discontinuous. To speak in the broadest terms used heretofore, the first Roman Ode addresses the timeless ordering of social life under heaven, and the second presents aspects of social life energized by *virtus* and mediated in art. The third Roman Ode sets forth collectivized society, the Roman state, in time, that is, in history: but in a historical process that the poet's vision makes open to artistic representation. Yet the *vates* who speaks the opening of III.1 remains the same; we have through the reading process come to a fuller grasp of him and of his concerns. And further, the audience specified for the cycle, the *virgines puerique* of III.1.4, still likewise obtains: if not youths themselves, at least a special of kind of audience, trained into competence by the process of the Roman Odes hitherto, and qualified by that openness and receptivity to what is new that characterizes children. Those childlike hearers of Horace will receive in III.3 not only exemplification of the *virtus* of III.2, but also a historical insight the fresh context of which only the untrammeled mind can receive. Out of the silence enjoined at the threshold of this monumental cycle speaks Juno's divine voice, addressing the Rome that the poet earlier addressed, and which he addresses throughout the sequence of the Roman Odes. Far from being a historical set-piece, or even retrospective in nature, Juno's long speech in III.3 breaks new ground precisely by virtue of its being set in this particular context: after society, life, *virtus* and art are set in motion, and before the great powers of poetry to fix, order and transmute are celebrated in III.4.

The conditions in which her speech finds itself, that is, proximately, the occasion of Romulus' being allowed by Juno to enter heaven, as well as the subsidiary conditions, such as the poems on each side of this dramatic scene in III.3, as just mentioned, constitute a repertory of formulaic thoughts, largely unstated, but nevertheless, through their order-

---

[1] *Supra*, n. 7, p. 7. On Odes III.3, see Eduard Fraenkel, *Horace* (Oxford: Oxford University Press, 1957), pp. 267ff., and Steele Commager, *The Odes of Horace* (New Haven: Yale University Press, 1962), pp. 110f., 209ff., 224f., and D. Pietrusinski, "L'Apothéose d'Auguste par rapport à Romulus—Quirinus," *Eos* 63 (1975), pp. 273-296.

ing, directing the reader's responses in certain ways, just as the sequence of a relief likewise orders his reactions. Let us begin by considering these conditions first as if the speech of Juno, and the rest of III.3, were being discovered for the first time by the reader who has reached only this point in his experience of the *Odes* (a strategem hitherto avoided in these pages) and subsequently as if the entire text of the Roman Odes were present at every moment in the reader's consciousness.

Most unequivocally, the *vir tenax propositi* of the poem's opening (III.3.1) is related to III.2.17-24, wherein *virtus* is defined and characterized first in civic terms (it knows not political defeat, and does not take up or put down the axes of authority at popular demand) just as in III.3.2 (the *civium ardor prava iubentium*). Likewise, the *virtus* of the second Roman Ode is further characterized in a more cosmic way (opening heaven to the meritorious) and in a real sense the third Roman Ode fully explores this, both in the form of the hand of flashing Jupiter (III.3.6) and most extensively in the speech of Juno on the enrolling of Quirinus, the divinized Romulus, in heaven, supposedly as an implementer of the *virtus* of III.2 and of the *propositum* of III.3. Further locales out of which grow important elements in III.3 include the implied collapse of a building in III.2.27ff., and the collapse of the world in III.3.7ff.; this latter event, whilst ostensibly referring to the natural world, may also, in view of III.3.2f. and III.2.17-24, have a political connotation: the *propositum* that sees one through is evidently a whole plan of life, not for the self merely, but as well for the public good. Political pressure, natural forces and the ultimate calamity of the world's end are all aspects of the testing of the *propositum*.

The wind and thunder of Jupiter in III.3.4ff. give way to Juno's speech in such a manner as inevitably to suggest the demonic storm of the first book of the *Aeneid*, with its concomitant political overtone, and the subsequent speech of Jupiter on future Roman greatness: a point to bear in mind when thinking of how the publication of the *Aeneid* five years after the appearance of Odes I-III would affect an audience's reading of Horace here.[2]

For mortals, advice is given at the outset of III.3 on how rulers (*tyrannus* again: specifically foreign, but probably generic in scope as well) and heaven itself should not shake one's resolve; this reprise of ordering set forth by III.1.5ff. now includes elements passing beyond *quod satis est*, viz., *iustitia* and *propositum*. They are characterized, again on the mortal level, by rigidity and inflexibility, tenacity at its best, indeed an *ars*, or

---

[2] *Aeneid* I.148ff. Note that the simile employs *vir gravis pietate et meritis*, and *ignobile volgus*. See M. C. J. Putnam, *The Poetry of the Aeneid* (Cambridge: Harvard University Press, 1966), pp. 10f.

techné, line nine. But the intransigency counselled in the first two strophes gives way with the mention of *ars* to a view of *hac arte* as a means to an end, flexible, and responsive as well, knowing when to concede, as does Juno in her great speech that is the magnificent divine *exemplum*, authenticating and qualifying the human advice. *Ars* here has its moral implications, and is not merely the product of *iustitia* and a *vir tenax propositi*.

The examples of implementers of this *ars* are Pollux, Hercules, Augustus, Bacchus and finally Quirinus (III.3.9-16). Each would have had a specific implication for the poem's audience, on several levels. Pollux, with his unnamed twin, is a guide and a messenger of Rome's military fortunes, and would be associated with a specific spot in the Roman Forum, the Temple of Castor and Pollux. He is closely associated with Roman history and with divine interest in Rome's well-being.[3] Hercules, the stoic saint par excellence, has a divine father as does Pollux; further, like Pollux he has close association with early Rome,[4] and as well a topographical association with the Aventine and with the Ara Maxima at the north-west end of the Circus Maximus at the Forum Boarium. Augustus, whose future in heaven is assumed (*bibet* can be the only likely reading)[5] is likewise intimately involved in making the state's history, has a number of specific topographical sites associated with himself, though not so many as after the publication of the Odes I-III, and by association, a divine parentage. The *igneas arcis* that he and his divine forebears achieve are very much the heavenly contrast of the *uda humus* of III.2.23f. and its political coloration or discoloration. Each of the figures mentioned in the third strophe of III.3, by adhering to *iustitia*, to his *propositum*, made Rome more secure and transcended the human sphere to which at least part of their birth-origins consigned them. Each likewise was tied to topographical monuments.

When we reach Bacchus, the reader faces a different kind of exemplum. Even if it is left diplomatically ambiguous in the three preceding strophes whether one struggles one's way to heaven (the implication of

---

[3] News of the Roman victory against the Latins at Lake Regillus in 496 B.C. was said to have been conveyed to Rome by Castor and Pollux, whose temple at the south-east end of the Forum Romanum was vowed that year, and consecrated in 484 B. C., at the spot they were seen watering their horses.

[4] E.g., Hercules slays Cacus, the monster of the Aventine, *Aeneid* VIII.194ff. He had two temples in Rome: Hercules Victor/Triumphalis, associated with the triumphal procession, at the Ara Maxima in the Forum Boarium, and, perhaps significantly for this passage of Horace, he was worshipped in a purely Roman form as Hercules Musarum in a temple by the Portico of Octavia in the Campus Martius.

[5] Kiessling-Heinze *ad loc.* term *bibit*, the other reading, "sachlich unmöglich": it is not much defended these days.

enisus, line ten) or whether heaven graciously bestows such a place (*patiar*, line thirty-six), nevertheless, neither category fits *Bacchus pater*. He was not always remembered as a god, but no lately-contrived apotheosis is being imposed on him here.[6] Rather, Bacchus serves to implement an aspect of *ars* somewhat different from its use hitherto in III.3: Bacchus' *ars* here consists in the taming of the tigers to draw his car. His divine power is made manifest over the wildest of beasts, remote and mysterious themselves.[7] This *ars*, rather than any apotheosis, is what draws him into this poem, anticipating, by that type of Horatian interlacing with which the reader of the whole cycle of Roman Odes is familiar, the power of art celebrated in the succeeding poem, III.4.

The odd syntax of III.3.13 signals this change in perspective and of subject from *enisus* and what follows (lines ten following) to *tigres*, line fourteen: from struggle to effortless manifestation of power controlled by divine will. The *hac* thrice repeated (lines nine, thirteen and fifteen) stresses the identity of the moral quality or property, and its ultimate connections with divine will, in all four of its manifestations, as well as in its epiphany in unmediated image of power, Bacchus drawn by tigers, and thus taken up into heaven.

Quirinus, like the others of strophes three and four, was of divine parentage; the son of Gradivus or Mars, he was taken up to heaven on his father's horses. In the context called into existence by Horace's four opening strophes, Quirinus functions as the proximate occasion of the goddess' speech, and as the culmination of a series of assertions that begins with an unnamed man, the *vir* of strophes one and two, progresses to the divine Pollux and Hercules, through the to-be-divine Augustus, and on to the long-divine Bacchus. Romulus/Quirinus redirects this group back to the order of the semi-divine, that is, to a personage with one divine parent; thus strophes three and four constitute a kind of pedi-

---

[6] Cf. Ovid, *Tristia* V.3.19: 'ipse quoque aetherias meritis invectus es arces, / quo non exiguo facta labore via est,' a traditional view of Bacchus. Convenient references to views of Bacchus as a mortal made god for his great achievements, i.e., inventing wine, in Stefan Weinstock, *Divus Julius* (Oxford: Oxford University Press, 1971), pp. 228, 356, and especially 357, on ascensions of mortals in his cult in Rome. No major sanctuary to Bacchus / Dionysus was dedicated in Rome. There was a Sacellum Bacchus on the Sacra Via near the south-west corner of the Basilica of Constantine, mentioned in Martial, IX.72 and represented on a coin of Antoninus Pius; it is not an early building.

[7] One should perhaps bear in mind that tigers had not yet been seen in Rome, making their appearance only in 11 B.C.: Pliny, *Natural History* VIII.68. The chariot of Dionysus, with a baldachin of columns and a roof, was associated with the cult of the dead Alexander, and was used at Julius Caesar's funeral; Weinstock, *op. cit. supra*, n. 6, p. 362; H. J. Mette, "Roma (Augustus) und Alexander," *Hermes* 88 (1960), pp. 458-462; A. R. Bellinger, "The Immortality of Alexander and Augustus," *Yale Classical Studies* 15 (1957), pp. 91-100.

ment, with Augustus at its apex, tied closely to an address of state (*consiliantibus divis,* lines seventeen and following)[8] by a major divinity, one of the Capitoline Triad.

Juno's speech is by no means tangentially related to its four-strophe introduction, though so sensitive a critic as Gordon Williams avers that "the whole circumstance of Romulus' entry into heaven comes to [the poet's] mind, as it were by accident."[9] Let us note that Juno's address begins with a negative example of what has been said up to now: Laomedon was not *iustus* nor was he *tenax propositi;* Paris gave his disastrous judgment about the goddesses when swayed by *ardor prava iubentium,* and his whole world, and that of Troy collapsed as a result (strophes five and six and seven paralleling strophes one and two). The close connection between Juno's remarks and their setting can also be seen on the lexical level. Our first clue is line twenty-eight, *refringit,* proceeding from line seven, *fractus;* here the ruin of Troy through perjury is verbally contrasted with the steadfastness of the just man in the face of his world's ruin. If *fractus* generates or develops *refringit,* so too does another phonic element dominate Juno's speech to the gods assembled, her major policy address: the sound *re* as initial syllable. No fewer than seven times does it introduce a verb (*refringit,* line twenty-eight; *resedit,* thirty; *redonabo,* thirty-three; *reparare,* sixty; *renascens,* sixty-one; *resurgit,* sixty-five, and, in the poem's concluding strophe, *referre,* seventy-one. Ten more times does the syllable itself occur: in Juno's speech, *Hectoreis,* line twenty-eight; *inire, discere/ducere,* thirty-four; *visere,* fifty-four; *rebus,* fifty-nine; *sorore,* sixty-four; and in the concluding strophe, *referre,* seventy-one and *tenuare,* seventy-two. The sound is likewise present in the strophes leading up to Juno's address, and at a most strategic place: the words associated with Augustus, *recumbens,* line ten, and *purpureo ore,* twelve, and with Bacchus, *vexere,* line fourteen.[10] The reverse of *re, -er,* seems also prominent in *iterabitur,* line sixty-two, and *ter ter ter* in sixty-five, sixty-six and sixty-seven.

The occurrence of *re* plus verb or *-re-* or *-re-* or *-er* seems unduly frequent to be accounted for by chance, especially in, say, the seven-line spread of lines twenty-eight to thirty-four, with its six occurrences. All of Juno's speech concerns what will happen or not happen if Rome repeats,

---

[8] See also Ennius, *Annales* I *passim* for evidence of such a council, and parallel expressions; note that in *Aeneid* I, Juno, who does not address the council there, is like Jupiter, who does, a member (along with Minerva) of the Capitoline Triad.

[9] Gordon Williams, *The Third Book of Horace's Odes* (Oxford: Oxford University Press, 1969), p. 43.

[10] I of course exclude the syllable *re-* plus consonant, e.g., *merentem,* line thirteen, or *ploret,* line sixty-eight.

recapitulates or rebuilds Troy, and the sound *re* has strong significance in such a context; indeed; it creates it. The sound *re* in Juno's speech is associated largely with the negative past, the present relinquishing of animosity, and the promise of its resumption if certain events recur. Likewise, Augustus' future, expressed through *recumbens / purpureo bibet ore nectar*, lines which more than one commentator has found "an error of taste and judgement,"[11] is drawn into the *re* network of Juno's speech and thus his future is likewise subject to the contingencies there set forth.

It has always been clear that Juno's speech in III.3 is thematically related to the progress of Rome's historical destiny. The present remarks serve merely to show the artistic basis for this link, and to demonstrate how the speech fits into the introductory assertions made by this ode. Augustus' future divine state is earned by being a co-founder of the new Rome along with the original founder of old Rome, Romulus, but it is also true that Augustus' future divinity is approved of, even if not explicitly granted or conceded, by Juno. The word *redonabo*, line thirty-three, in its religious sense of pardon, remit, condone, with implications of expiation and atonement, is of course to be construed with Augustus as much as with Quirinus, although the poet does not, for social or political expediency, stress this point at strophe three when Augustus is named. The bases for Juno's concession in past and future form the bulk of her speech. It should be carefully noted that the implacable circularity of her announcement, as in lines sixty-five following, "ter si resurgat murus aeneus, / ... ter pereat," has a structural parallel in the last segment of her address, line sixty-eight, with the first line of the poem. Both exhibit *virum*. But in light of Juno's negative assertions, what has happened to the human optimism and self-faith exhibited in strophes one and two? Obviously the reader who reaches the last but one of the poem's strophes will cause the initial assertions to undergo serious qualification in his mind. The line of thought may be said to go something like this: A man, *vir*, may be *tenax propositi*, as in rebuilding Troy; he may be guiltless, even *iustus*, but if he is linked to a flawed enterprise, he is doomed. Compare this to III.2.29f.: "saepe Diespiter / neglectus incesto addidit integrum." If the foe of certain historical forces,[12] he is likewise to perish. Those who keep the faith and who win and are eligible to be granted heaven are on "the right side"; one cannot be *tenax propositi* in the face of divine opposition, for then one's *propositum* is surely flawed.

---

[11] E.g., Williams, *op. cit. supra*, n. 9, p. 42; on the suddenness of the parenthetical structure, p. 16.

[12] It is interesting to observe that Juno in the *Aeneid* is an anti-historical force, striving to obviate "what happened," but plays no such rôle in Horace *Odes* III.3.

Troy's *dux fraudulentus* (line twenty-four) led his people to ruin; the guiltless suffered, and will suffer along with the guilty. Rome's original *dux* was Romulus, now, by the speech-action of Juno, or in other words by the speech-act of *Odes* III.3, enrolled in heaven as Quirinus. Rome's present *dux* is far from his hour of translation to heaven, but, following the conditions of III.3, he too can be eligible for reward if he is not found to be on the wrong side, if he is not *tenax* of a *propositum* that is divinely opposed. Juno herself is conceivably the tyrant of III.3.3, asking what some in the poem's audience surely would consider *prava*, namely to be not *nimium pii*, line fifty-eight, to give up too easily old positions and convictions, either of hostility to the Republicans who killed Julius Caesar (now Divus Julius himself), or of hostility to the winners by the losers. The quality of *pietas* is not in question, however; its object is. The *vir* whom his family is moved to mourn at the end of the speech, lines sixty-seven and following, is the *vir* of the ode's opening, but now an Antony-like figure, the man "on the wrong side."

The founders, Romulus/Quirinus and Augustus are, in this text, linked along the level of function, i.e., obviously founder, and keeper of faith with the people and with the gods; they are also linked by Juno, who times the event in regard to Quirinus with the rare word *elocuta*, line seventeen, and so, underscoring this verbal action which thus draws attention to itself, gives a time context for the event in the poem, and for the present Roman world heeding that poem. What was a series of past exempla of the poet's aphorism, *attigit*, line ten, *vexere*, fourteen, *fugit*, sixteen, penetrated by a future assertion made in the light of the past actions, *bibet*, line twelve, becomes with *elocuta Iunone*, lines seventeen and following, time present, the time of her speech, which ends hostilities and admits Quirinus to the divine company, and does not merely recall or project doing so.

One may, but need not, see detailed political references in Juno's allusion to the guilty of fallen Troy, the enemies of Augustus, say, in the operations of Paris, the ghost of Cleopatra VII in the foreign woman, in strophe seven; what is central is the remote origin (*ex quo,* line twenty-one) of Juno's affront,[13] and her injunction to recognize that the past is the past (*iam nec,* line twenty-five). Indeed, it needs to be emphasized that Juno's address explicitly cautions against looking back: she condones and forgives on that condition, and it is one of grave importance for the consolidation of the Roman state and its future by its present ruler Augustus.

---

[13] Cf. Vergil, *Georgics* I.502: 'satis iam pridem sanguine nostro / Laomedonteae luimus periuria Troiae'; cf. M. C. J. Putnam, *Virgil's Poem of the Earth* (Princeton: Princeton University Press, 1979), pp. 73-76.

The civic quality of these metaphors used by the poet to describe Quirinus' achieving heaven coterminously with Juno's pronouncing *redonabo* (line thirty-three) underscores the poem's direction of civil life: religion allows the working out of the processes of the state; *discere* and *adscribi* both come from such processes of civil life as the formal enrollment in a tribe or other group.[14] What was done *hac arte* (line nine) before Juno's speech act, and hence on an individualized basis, without her sanction, even if for the civic group, becomes achieved *hac lege* (line fifty-eight); one notes the identical position in the line of both phrases. The collectivized *lex* (assented to by many if promulgated by one) replaces or makes fulfilled the individualized *ars*. Rome may give laws and fill the world with her presence, and spurn the wealth that belongs to the gods, on condition that the past not be revisited or set in operation once again. It would be too particularizing of this allusive text to say that the poet here discourages a return to power of the *optimates*, or too great foreign influence; the point is in the poem's terms, however, not too broad to have some specific meaning.

It has already been remarked that the poem's syntax grows complicated at the mention of Bacchus, who himself fits imperfectly into the chain of examples the poet sets forth in that he alone does not have a cult center in Rome. It should also be pointed out that a similar dislocation of syntax occurs in Juno's speech, lines forty-nine following. The idea about gold undetected "et sic melius situm," and what follows, does not perfectly fit into the civic and military vision purveyed by the goddess' prophecy of Rome's destiny. She links the human and the divine worlds together on an individual basis, viz., the infinitive *spernere* is unusually made to modify the adjective *fortior*, which, whilst ostensibly signifying Rome, must in the context of the Roman Odes heretofore read signify as well an individual Roman, one who is stronger to look askance at wealth than to secularize the sacred for his own gain. The state becomes the citizen, a point also made by Vergil in his *Aeneid*. The noteworthy syntax sets forth this noteworthy idea, just as it signalled a break in the parallelism in the heroic examples when it reached Bacchus, line thirteen.

The eighteenth strophe of III.3 breaks away from Juno's speech abruptly,[15] on the grounds of literary convention: the speech of gods does

---

[14] *Adscribere* is the technical word for such enrollment.

[15] Pindar as stylistic example for Horace could be cited in many connections; suffice it to note here *Pythian* 11.41 and 10.5 for abrupt breaks such as here. Cf. J. H. Waszink, "Horace und Pindar," *Antike und Abendland* 12 (1966), pp. 111-124; C. W. Whitaker, "A Note on Horace and Pindar," *Classical Quarterly* 50 (1956), pp. 221-224, and E. L. Highbarger, "The Pindaric Style of Horace," *Transactions and Proceedings of the American Philological Association* 66 (1955), pp. 222-255, especially pp. 235-241 on the Roman Odes; he believes that III.3 and III.4 are the most Pindaric.

not accord with a lyric meter (*iocosa lyra*, line sixty-nine). By this tactic, Horace redirects the reader's attention to the fact that a speech-act has been in progress, and that a poem or poetic cycle is still underway, one which is about to seek a new direction away from heaven (*Descende caelo* of III.4.1 in this sense). He also reinserts his own persona, which will dominate III.4, and which has been lost to sight since the end of III.2.26ff., *vetabo* and what follows. In this fashion Horace modulates the reader's attention away from epic expectations and concomitant prophecies and visions of Rome's greatness, and back to the fabric of the artistic event itself: the text. This is further signalled by the occurence of *pervicax*, line seventy, an ancient word not usual in the contemporary language, and reminiscent in its unusualness of *elocuta*, line seventeen; both bracket Juno's speech with an emphasis on its ancient historicity and on its textuality, its poetic and hence verbal-action aspects.

But by using the future tense, *conveniet*, line sixty-nine, the poet leaves hanging in the air unstated what Juno would have said, or "was about to say" when Horace ceases to transmit her words. Would what she have said been bad for Rome? By leaving the goddess gesturing towards what lies outside our field of vision, the poet takes leave of her, and has us do the same, with all her power and mystery intact. We cannot know what else Juno may have said, but we have the succeeding Roman Odes, and rudiments of an awareness of the apocopated speech's negative dimensions. Rome will fall again, indeed is falling, if in reading Juno's speech the reader also has read III.6. It is of the utmost significance that III.3 ends in a breakdown of reference: Juno's future words are to be about objects that do not (yet?) exist, and may, through right action, be aborted.

In the shaping of moral values from *quod satis est* (III.1) to individual glory, individual death and individual faith-keeping (III.2) to the authentication and validation of individual actions (those of the *vir tenax*, Hercules, Augustus, Quirinus) by a divine power that lifts them to the level of the national (Rome, Troy) and supra-historical (*ex quo, iam nec, ter, ter, ter*) the poet has moved from self (a kind of pastoral self at the end of III.1 especially) to civic responsibility. He began the cycle as a hierophantic poet, and it remains for him in III.4 to reexamine the *virtus* of art from his own historical standpoint, and to reintegrate himself into the fabric of gods, men and time that has been set up in *Odes* III.1-3. For now, the audience which has not read III.4-6, the rest of the cycle, Juno's injunctions seem capable of being kept, and the outlook for Rome's future is bright. For those who have gone on to finish the cycle, however, her words betoken the internalized return to past ways of selfish hedonism, and the breakdown of the family, whose unperverted values shine forth in III.3.67f. Here civic calamity is the setting for private or individual

CHAPTER SIX

THE FOURTH ROMAN ODE

The fourth Roman Ode raises a host of questions. Not the least of these is its relationship to the conclusion of the third Roman Ode. The poet there asked, "quo, Musa, tendis?" (III.3.70) and the opening words of III.4, "Descende caelo," can be taken to signify a request that the Muse come back "down to earth" after drifting into elevated epical discourse with the speech of Juno in III.3. Without some bearing on III.3, even if not the one suggested, the opening strophe of III.4 seems too vague to be purposeful. If taken to mean, engage in choral ode (implied by *tibia*) or in lyric monody (implied by *fidibus citharave*) rather than in epic, the opening serves as a bridge from III.3 to III.4, from the end of the first three odes to the beginning of the final triad. Thus it is appropriate for sound to dominate this new beginning (the voice and musical instruments of strophe one, and the haunting "auditis?... audire et videor" of the second) just as silence was invoked in III.1.1ff. Further, just as III.1 dealt with the poet's self (largely by reverse implication) so too III.4 dwells for seven strophes on the person of the poet. But III.4 stands alone among the Roman Odes in regard to severe problems of transition, sequence of images and indeed in constituting a permissible range of interpretation. These problems (and there are others) are foreshadowed by the fluid blending of the end of III.3 into the opening of III.4, and intensified by the highly ambiguous *audire et videor pios / errare per lucos*. Such difficulties also are met in trying to relate the local settings of Apulia to both the rôle of art as it transpires in strophes ten and eleven, and to the gigantomachy (strophes twelve through seventeen) and its mournful aftermath (strophes eighteen through twenty). The gnome "vis consili expers mole ruit sua" is also hard-put to assume a governing function for the whole ode (line sixty-five).

Instead of recapitulating the often successful suggestions for dealing with the disparate elements of III.4,[1] a radical approach to reading this

---

[1] On III.4 see Eduard Fraenkel, *Horace* (Oxford: Oxford University Press, 1957), pp. 273ff., and Steele Commager, *The Odes of Horace* (New Haven: Yale University Press, 1962), pp. 194ff. The only textual difficulty of moment is in line ten: *Apuliae* or *Pulliae*; for a persuasive stand in favor of the province instead of the personal name (the latter favored by Klingner) see David O. Ross, Jr., *Backgrounds to Augustan Poetry* (Cambridge: Cambridge University Press, 1975), p. 145, n.1. For a discussion of the question favoring *Pulliae*, see A. Treloar, "Horace, Odes III.4.10," *Antichthon* 2 (1968), pp. 58-62. A detailed examination (in German) of III.4 is I. Borzsák, "Descende caelo...," *Acta Antiqua Academiae Scientiarum Hungaricae* 8 (1960), pp. 369-386. For the political ramifications,

text is put forward here in the hope that it will enable readers to see that other categories for testing and experiencing a highly complex Horatian ode are available besides the well-tried unity of subject, tone, approach, theme, and so on. This novel reading, or better, method for reading the text does not seek to disestablish the older methods of interpreting this ode, but rather only to supplement them with a method of reading this ode that does not seem as yet advanced for reading Roman poetry.

In reading any poetic text of more than minimal length, the reader is often obliged by cultural and institutional expectations to consider the text as continuous, proceeding from beginning to close without ceasing to be a text. Classicists are educated to believe that an amount of reading coterminous with a book of an epic poem, roughly 1,000 lines at the maximum, is the amount ideally "taken in" during one "reading" by the ancient reading audience. Those who teach Greek and Latin are all too familiar with the problem of discontinuity of the reading experience of a classical text in the class room: a book of the *Aeneid* or an act of a comedy of Plautus is slowly decoded at a rate which insures the total disappearance of anything approximating its original impact on a native speaker of Latin. Through this slowing down of the rate of consumption, certain problems appear or are made to appear,[2] and other problems, or better, phenomena, vanish from our gaze as we claw our way from sentence to sentence. Only shorter poems such as Horace's *Odes* or Catullus' polymetrics or elegies are sufficiently graspable in a time-frame for reading anything like that generated by the text in its ancient setting. The fourth Roman Ode, the longest of the cycle, presents twenty strophes, an extent of text that is not too long for synthesizing in modern times an ancient time-frame for reading, say approximately seven minutes for reading the whole ode aloud, with pauses, and with comprehension of it in most cases assumed by prior study of it. It is precisely this ability to grasp the whole poem that occasions the modern perception that the poem is unintegrated. A book of Vergil's *Aeneid* or of Lucretius does not invite this observation because of its length: the experiencing mind of the reader, especially a modern reader not at home with oral presentation of poetry, and dependent on easy access to text through the codex format, cannot keep before itself such a wealth of perceptions as that provided in a thousand hexameter lines. But it can and should retain

---

see J. Aymard, "La Politique d'Auguste et l'ode III.4 d'Horace," *Latomus* 15 (1956), pp. 26-36; D. A. Malcolm, "Horace *Odes* III.4," *Classical Review* N. S. 5 (1955), pp. 242-244; A. J. Dunston, "Horace *Odes* III.4 and the Virtues of Augustus," *AUMLA* 31 (1969), pp. 9-19, and R. A. Hornsby, "Horace on Art and Politics (Ode 3.4)," *Classical Journal* 58 (1962), pp. 97-104, especially p. 102 on Horace's use of time.

[2] Cf. George Duckworth, *The Nature of Roman Comedy* (Princeton: Princeton University Press, 1952), p. viii and pp. 198ff.

simultaneous perceptions of twenty Alcaic strophes, a matter of eighty short lines.

It should be obvious that large poems (like large buildings, or lengthy cinematic films) are discovered (or, on re-experiencing, rediscovered) at every moment, whilst short poems (like small art structures) are entirely present and available at every moment when being addressed. This is not to say that rediscovery of *interpretation* does not occur in rereading a short poem, but that uncovering or discovery or rediscovery of *text* occurs in a longer poem, whereas the mind of the audience experiencing a shorter text has that text (even imperfectly) before it at every moment of experiencing a segment of that text. Hence it follows that when we "remember" *Oedipus Rex* (even if, *a fortiori,* we have committed the text of it to memory) we are remembering a different order of artistic phenomenon than when we "remember" Catullus' couplet "Odi et amo," even if we cannot perfectly recollect the order of the distich's words. Much work needs to be done to set limits to what may be called a short poem and what may be called a long poem, both for us and for ancient society.

But even before such exact inquiry takes place, certain assertions of some use to the student of literature might be made about a poem like Horace *Odes* III.4. Once one has attentively "read through" this text, subsequent attentive or competent rereadings of it will oblige the reader to make an effort to discover the text anew at each strophe, in other words, to discard strophes one and two at the outset of the third, to jettison the first five at "vester, Camenae," line twenty-one, etc. From what we know about how poets of much longer works proceeded, and what they expected their audiences to bring to the text experience, we know this effort of discarding or forgetting was not encouraged. Even attentive readers of long epics were presumably expected and able to respond to the nudging parallels triggering recollection, catalogued by modern scholars.[3] The lyric poet on the other hand capitalizes and improves upon the capacity of his audience to have the entire text available at every moment whilst as it were inhabiting the text. Hence discontinuity of theme, for instance, is a frustration of a legitimate expectation on the part of a competent audience. The discontinuities of Horace *Odes* III.4 are of more moment, aesthetically, than are the multiple ranges of subject in a book of Lucretius, because of size of text, or in an epistle or satire of

---

[3] E.g., M. C. J. Putnam, *The Poetry of the Aeneid* (Cambridge: Harvard University Press, 1966), pp. 95f. on the relationship of *Aeneid* V. 836f. to III.511 and II.250ff.: correspondences presumed to occur to a reader using a papyrus roll. Cf. J. Balogh, "Voces Paginarum," *Philologus* 82 (1926-27), pp. 84-109.

Horace, because of generic incitings of expectation.[4] The present age equates size with monumentality, with all of the complex organization, subordination, symmetry, parallelism and totality of interpretation that the term "monumental" implies; it might be useful (in another context) to test to see if our modern predeliction for linking size with seriousness, with monumentality, has any validity in ancient works. Callimachus assumed that length and seriousness were linked; but surely Apuleius' *Metamorphosis* and Petronius' *Satyricon* (to name prose works) *need* not be complexly ordered because of the fact of their being long; need the *Aeneid*?

As for the fourth Roman Ode, its relatively small scope should not blind us to its architectonic virtuosity; if the Casa Romuli can be seen as the adumbration of the Basilica Ulpia,[5] there is no cause for surprise if an ode of Horace display "monumental" features.

Before turning finally to the world of texts in language, another observation concerning the architecture that uses tangible materials may be permitted. Roman architecture tended to make continuously available to its beholder or inhabitant the whole fabric of space. His whereabouts is consistently made known in relation to the whole through the axiality of the given structure. Anomalies like the Pantheon or the probably imperial villa at Piazza Armerina achieve no small measure of their strong effects by foiling the expectations of their beholders. Buildings which have no place for the observer,[6] like the Pantheon of Hadrian, or which are discovered moment by moment like Domitian's palace on the Palatine or the fourth-century villa at Piazza Armerina, or buildings, like Sulla's Fortuna Primigenita at Praeneste, which take over and control the reactions and movements of those experiencing the structure: these buildings are relatively rare, late, or Near Eastern in tone. Roman poems like Roman architecture—even long poems or big buildings— try to present a place for their audiences and, when small in scope, to make themselves wholly available to their audiences at every moment of experiencing their fabric. The fourth Roman Ode goes out of its way not to do this.

An aspect of Roman architecture and art most closely linked to the Roman Odes in terms of civic function, monumentality, and total availability to the audience is the Roman historical relief. Like a poem, a relief is "read," has conventions of vocabulary and expression and hence varying competencies of audience, and presents varying interpretations

---

[4] On unity in Horatian satire, see the present writer's *Latin Satire* (Leiden, 1970), pp. 61f.

[5] Cf. Frank E. Brown, *Roman Architecture* (New York, 1967), pp. 11 and 34. The buildings are of course related through the concept of axiality that is central to Roman architecture.

[6] This to be sure is not the case of Augustan classicism in buildings.

and significances layered upon one other. Like poetry, reliefs are highly dependent upon context; the collocations of Horace *Odes* I.35, III.24 and the Roman Odes[7] are different in no way (save that of the difference between topography on land and topography in a verbal text) from the positioning of the *Ara Pietatis Augustae* and the *Ara Pacis Augustae* in their urban topographical contexts.[8] Like poetry, reliefs are "read" in a sequence of images which is emphatically not the sequence of interpretation or significance.

Perhaps the chief difference between classical poetry and that composed from the Renaissance until very recently is that the order of words in a classical poem is not the same thing as the order of meaning, because of the nature of the ancient inflected languages and their syntax. Reference to ancient art, especially to historical relief, which comes closest to a modern sequential "narrative" style, should show that interpretation is afforded by the accumulation of detail, by context, and by considering the work as existing wholly in the present moment of experience; what is "on the back" of an altar is simultaneously present when we view its front.[9]

It would be erroneous to assign the same mode of existence to a plastic work of art like the *Ara Pacis Augustae* and to a poem of Horace. Yet in many cases the same audience read both historical relief and text. The modes of consumption of both the historical relief and the progression of the text's words may be more closely related than is now surmised, and even a cursory examination of how we read a relief may throw light on how we are invited to read a Horatian ode. First of all, the import of a relief is not to be tied to the content of its scenes or to the order in which the scenes unfold. In a late example, but stylistically close to the *Ara Pacis Augustae*, the Emperor Domitian in the Cancelleria reliefs is accompanied by divinized personifications of the City and its people and simultaneously by Mars and Minerva.[10] It is assumed that the scenes, while sequen-

---

[7] *Supra*, pp. 8ff.

[8] The situation of the two altars on opposite sides of the city, at gates with important symbolic implications, must be part of a coherent Augustan program, even though the *Ara Pietatis Augustae* was vowed only in 22 A.D. and built in 43 A.D. Mario Torelli, *Typology and Structure of Roman Historical Reliefs* (Ann Arbor: The University of Michigan Press, 1982), pp. 66-82.

[9] See e.g., the altar of Manlius, in the Lateran collection now housed in the Vatican Museum, in Inez Scott Ryberg, *Rites of the State Religion in Roman Art* (*Memoirs of the American Academy in Rome* 22 (1955), pp. 84-87 and plates 25 and 26. Also Torelli, *op. cit. supra*, n. 8, pp. 16-19, and Plates I.6, I.7 and I.8. It is obvious that the viewer of this altar is to keep in mind the reliefs of all four sides in order to make the altar "represent" its interpretation.

[10] I. S. Ryberg, *op. cit. supra*, n. 9, pp. 75-80 on the Cancelleria reliefs, also in the Vatican Museum.

tial, are more than a narration of linearly progressive discrete events. Assertions are made about the emperor, his policies, his problems, his relations with heaven, and a great many other things. The audience is directly involved, supplies responses, fills, through its awareness of experiences beyond the relief (and through awareness of other reliefs) the various lacunae that occur, and otherwise discharges its function of interpreting the conventions of historical reliefs, the least of which conventions is the yoking of interpretation to the sequence of observations. Rather, multiplicity of interpretation is secured by simultaneous experience of the whole rather than of the parts: a fact which enables the relatively accurate restoration of reliefs that have lost some of their sequences, a task generally beyond present literary scholarship to discharge for an extensively damaged text with comparable likelihood of correctness.

A grasp of the interpretive force of the *Ara Pacis Augustae* comes from getting beyond a reading that contents itself with "next to Agrippa comes X and then Y and Z." One only misses dealing with a cause by such descriptions of effects. Likewise, one does not assess the fourth Roman Ode by observing that remarks on the poet's personal life are succeeded by a gigantomachy. Since words are inevitably referential, and since to be intelligible even on the referential level they must be assigned to temporal sequence dictated by grammar and syntax, we naturally tend to perceive the text as a series of observations rather than as a *summa* governed by a *lex*, like the *Ara Pacis Augustae*, a total monument with its *lex arae*. The individual processions on the altar, representing the vowing of its construction, are like the wings of a given text, or the Roman Ode sequence as a whole, recognizable as a series of individuals, portraits even, high in referential qualities, but when "in the monument" or "in the text" subordinated to a greater interpretation, and full of self-reference: peace, watchfulness, balance, oikoumene, or whatever other interpretation the monument affords. The recognizable individual elements of a poem or a poem cycle (words, sentences, images or metaphors, events, moods, orderings) must be seen as likewise subordinate to the monument to which they refer and which they and they alone constitute, and which they, in sequence and in context, serve to interpret. The whole is neither coterminous with its parts nor is it detachable from them. We have less trouble freeing monuments such as the *Ara Pacis Augustae* from the tyranny of sequential reading, but it might be worth the trouble to attack a poem such as III.4 from this kind of perspective.

Such an approach would avoid procedures which aim at revealing what the poem "is about" and would instead stress function and effect on the reader's consciousness both as the poem progresses and as a static whole.

In its aspects as a *summa*, the poem inculcates awareness of the power of order over chaos, and the power of art over random event. The central exemplum of this is the gigantomachy, into which Horace has introduced certain idiosyncratic elements, for reasons to be discussed presently. The pinnacle of the power structure in the world mediated by III.4 is Jupiter in lines forty-two and following. Here his past victory over the Titans and the hateful band of the forces of disorder is set forth, as well as his present complete sway over earth, sea and underworld, with their human and divine inhabitants. The tenses of *sustulerit*, on the one hand, and of *temperat* and *regit* on the other (lines forty-four, forty-five and forty-eight) show the subordination of the past demonstration of power to present domination; the tenses of *intulerat, possent, stetit*, presenting past exampla (lines forty-nine and fifty-eight), and *lavit* and *tenet* presenting present (but possibly not eternal) action and control (lines sixty-one and sixty-two), mirror this sequence. What is paramount is what is present: Jupiter and Apollo share the present tense. One rules through power, the other through art, and the gnome of line sixty-five re-unites the two elements: power bereft of judgment (*consilium*) falls to destruction. We have seen as much just before the great picture of Jupiter with the universe in his sway: the Muses at line forty-one give judgment (*consilium* again) just as they refresh Caesar Augustus, wielder of civic powers as extensive as Jupiter's divine power, and similarly threatened by enemies. The Muses too inhabit the present tense (*recreatis, datis*, lines forty and forty-one); they too, like Apollo, their closest celestial connection, form present-day exempla for the assertion that the god governs and rules.

If one were fancifully to conjure up a relief representing the leading ideas of this by no means accidentally centered section of the fourth Roman Ode, one might expect to see a Jupiter dominating the three areas of the universe: first earth, with the goddess Terra (sometimes iden-tified as Italia) lamenting the loss of her sons who stormed heaven (lines seventy-three and following, with analogy to the civil wars). One might also picture here the poet protected by his Muses as a child, from the fall-ing tree, at Philippi (the civil war again), and saved at Cape Palinurus; further we would see his journeys to various remote spots (lines nine following). These same Muses might be seen sustaining Caesar Augustus, lines thirty-seven following. Next, Jupiter would be presented as controlling as well the sea, which would have already figured in the scenes of Baiae, Philippi, Cape Palinurus, the Bosphorus, Britain, etc.: the oikoumene of the divinity's power would be analogous to the so-called "Italia" of the *Ara Pacis Augustae*.[11] As for Jupiter's control over the

---

[11] This figure, variously called *Terra Mater* and *Italia*, probably a figure of *Oikoumene*, is on the west end of the *Ara Pacis Augustae*. Torelli, *op. cit. supra*, n. 8, pp. 40-42.

gloomy kingdoms, at this point could come a great balancing of the scenes representing the poet in the underworld, the powerful opening of the ode, and the concluding scenes presenting the fate of those challenging Jupiter's power and order, lines sixty-nine following. The fight of the gods versus the giants and the triumph of *consilium* would make a lively scene as well, and could be allied in placing or context as well as through gesture to the Muses and the superordinance of their *consilium*. Those familiar with Augustan art could easily work out such a representation of themes. Imagined in this fashion, even hypothetically, the ode may be seen to be unified and indeed as unified as any large Augustan civic historical relief.

To return to the realm of literary text: Horace, in the Roman Odes, presents a dazzling parade of ways to write a poem. The first in the cycle, we have seen, exhibits a unifying principle in the centrality of divine power, but presents as well a centrifugal model of a world fleeing that power. The first ode of the second half of the cycle, III.4, presents that power as challenged, but only in the time-frame of the past: Antony and the giants, who are themselves gone, but who call to mind other forces still capable of menace, opponents of Augustus' aims, and Etna itself. This last image is presented in a form that admits little self-congratulation on danger avoided: the swift fire has not (*perēdit*) eaten through superimposed Etna; the similarity with *Furor Impius* (*Aeneid* I.294ff.) who is chained but striving to break loose, is to be noted.[12] Both sinister figures may break their restraints at some future time.

Coherence and unity (to assume for the argument that they are desirable ends) can be achieved in a wide variety of ways by a skilled poet. In his fourth Roman Ode, Horace relies upon a dominating idea, *consilium* imported from a superior power to an inferior order, and attending ideas about the power of art to impose order. This idea is worked out in images or scenes that are disparate: the poet's childhood in a rural locale hitherto ungraced by mention in poetry; Titans assulting heaven; Caesar Augustus, probably adduced in connection with his triple triumph of 29 B.C., receiving advice from the voices of literature; the underworld punishment of those who bring violence against order. These almost emblematic scenes could occur serially without raising serious objection in Roman plastic art, whereas in poetry we expect unity of theme, orderly transition, and logical, dialectically linear progression of thought. How much Horace must we read to cease to be surprised at the verve with which he violates, purposefully and comprehensibly, these expectations? Yet there are clues to orderly development; for instance, the

---

[12] Cf. M. C. J. Putnam, *op. cit. supra*, n. 3, pp. 17f.

operative word *consilium* appears at line forty-one, just before the picture that the poet presents of the Titans threatening Jupiter's rule. It appears again, as before in the first half of a line opening a strophe, namely line sixty-five, in the gnomic passage mentioned earlier. Framed by this repetition is the only picture which the poet presents as shared by him and his audience: *scimus*, line forty-two. Here the first person plural represents those whom he addresses as well as the Muses, whom he has been unambiguously addressing, lines twenty-one and following. Muses, audience and poet are bound together in the great enunciation of the power of heaven's rule.

The other non-third person plural verb in the poem is *auditis*, in the form of a question at line five. The traditional explanations are that the poet addresses here either the boys and girls of III.1.4, or the Muses themselves, who later appear in the plural, as just seen. Yet a third possibility exists: *auditis* is addressed to us, the audience, much as *scimus*, line forty-one, subsumes the audience as well as the Muses. If the opening of the text be perceived as a process, one can see how the prayer, stressing auditory elements such as *dic, tibia, melos, voce acuta, fidibus, cithara*, is immediately fulfilled[13] with attendant sound: *auditis? audire videor*. He asks the normal question when one hears someone or something to which one cannot quite give credence: "Do you hear this? I seem to hear…" Subsequently the poet penetrates the Muses' territory, the *pii luci*, and goes on to present his antecedent credentials in strophes three and following. The unspecified sound that he hears at the poem's outset (unspecified save that it is an appropriate Muse-associated response, but we cannot say which, if any, of the musical choices presented in the first strophe the Muse or Muses implemented) grows more defined at the center panel of the text, the fight against the giants. In connection with this, are we to assume that the poet recalls both the struggle with the Titans (lines forty-two following) and with the giants (forty-nine following) or that he confused them?[14] At any rate, sound here again appears for the second and final time in the poem: the *sonantem Palladis aegida*, line fifty-seven.

The musical associations of Apollo are transferred to the sounds made by the aegis of Pallas, the ringing bronze of which reacts to the onslaught of mindless destructive force with a not unmusical clangor that accom-

---

13 So Kiessling-Heinze *ad loc.*

14 Kronos, parent of Zeus, was the leader of the Titans, of whom Horace's Iapetus (*Odes* I.3.27) is one; the conventional list of them is in Hesiod, *Theog.* 132ff. For the giants per se, F. Vian, "La guerre des géants devant les penseurs de l'antiquité," *Revue des Études Grecques* 65 (1952), pp. 1ff. On the battle of the giants signifying in Augustan poetry in general the struggle of Augustus against enemies, see V. Buchheit, "Mythos und Geschichte in Ovids Metamorphosen," *Hermes* 94 (1966), pp. 80-108.

panies the alarm engendered by the aegis itself. Order is restored through *consilium*, the content of judgment prevailing over the emptiness of brute force, but accompanied nevertheless by art, music, or poetry such as this ode.[15] Apollo is assigned a triple set of descriptive clauses (lines sixty and following) just as was Jupiter (lines forty-five and following). Two of the clauses describing both gods are *qui*-clauses, and each god has the last line of one strophe and the whole of the next devoted to him. Far from being a poem of personal lyric grafted onto Pindar's *First Pythian*,[16] this poem is a hymn of praise to God's rule, a more open structure adumbrated by the relatively closed Ode III.1. The power of heaven is coterminous with the power of art; Jupiter and Apollo share equal status in this monument. Their enemies were such as to inspire fear: Jupiter quakes before the onset of the warring giants, line forty-nine, and Apollo, together with Pallas, Vulcan and Juno (a grouping also reminiscent of the *Aeneid*) fights for order and imposes it through art, skill, and judgment. *Vis temperata*, the yoking of energy with mind, is what these paradigms inculcate, both on the level of poetic composition and the poetic persona, strophes three through nine, the sphere of political life wherein reflection and clement forebearance purveyed by aid of literature have rôles (strophe ten), as well as in the cosmic struggles of Titans and giants (strophes eleven through sixteen), and in its calmer illustrations of the poet's thesis (strophes seventeen through twenty).

The humble and obscure origins of the poet at the outset of III.4, along with his unstated responsibilities, may find a parallel in the giant Gyges of line sixty-nine, whose crime is unspecified,[17] and in Pirithous, not even a giant but simply a Lapith who accompanied Theseus on his mission to seize and remove Proserpina from the underworld, and who, unlike the poet in his projected safe wanderings, was caught and kept against his will: like the humble origins of Horace, a believable picture more susceptible of being understood in human terms than the gigantomachy.

Balance, progression and order are easily discerned in the text of the fourth Roman Ode. But the balance is symmetric and one of opposites, e.g., the music of art, the ringing bronze of the aegis, and not the static balance of similarities. Further, the progression is not linear but through a kind of multiple perodicity, wherein the time of the Titans becomes the

---

[15] On the concept of *consilium* broadly considered, see H. Lott, *Consilium: Versuch einer semasiologischer Darstellung des Begriffes für die Zeit der römischer Republik unter Berücksichtigung von Vergil und Horaz*, Diss. Freiburg, 1959.

[16] Gordon Williams, *The Third Book of Horace's Odes* (Oxford: Oxford University Press, 1969), p. 53. This has also been persuasively linked to Hesiod's *Theogony*; see A. H. F. Thornton, "Horace's Ode to Calliope," *AUMLA* 23 (1965), pp. 96-102.

[17] See Kiessling-Heinze on Horace *Odes* II.17.13; cf. Callimachus, *Del.* 141.

time of the giants' attempted take-over; the triumphs of Augustus Caesar
in 29 B.C., the poet's childhood in the decades of the 60's and 50's, the
time of hypothetical trips to the frontiers of empire and the time served in
underworld servitude are all simultaneously present. Order in III.4 is
that of complementary bi-polarities, force bereft of judgment and force
informed by judgment; the god of poetry musically fighting for universal
order, and the poet of the gods pugnaciously musical on behalf of political
stability. Pindar's *First Pythian* may well have provided the grand outlines
(music, personal victory, military victory, a new city's foundation, har-
monious governance) but it was Horace's genius to seize the impetus of
Roman art and to yoke opposites into a superb composition comparable
in technique and result to achievements in civic historical artistic programs in sculpture and relief.[18]

There is no key to this ode, no one fruitful approach to reading it, save
to be open to the impacts it makes serially upon the mind as one progressively consumes it, to watch one's expectations being thwarted or
outwitted or forestalled, and, bearing in mind its wholeness like a
familiar monument or space shaped by architecture, give oneself up to
the local effects in their total context. Jupiter's struggle and success
thereby informs Augustus' and the poet's as well; art is a driving force for
quelling chaos and keeping disorder beyond the frontiers of civilization
and of consciousness itself. The *amabilis insania,* the coining of the word
temptator (line seventy-one, after the Greek πειραστής, "assailant"), the
confining of Roman names to the strophes leading up to Caesar, and the
confining (except for strophe one) of Greek names to the strophes subsequent, the formal parallels in triadic units of contrasting pairs in the
description of Jupiter, and the cumulative triad characterizing Apollo, all
this drawing of attention to the surface texture of the poem, together with
its being the longest of the Roman Odes, results in its proclaiming of
itself as verbal artifice: one of those enunciations or musical sounds that
keep the dangers of blindness and unchanneled force at bay.

---

[18] See also the sculpture program for the temple of Mars Ultor, an important Augustan
project.

CHAPTER SEVEN

THE FIFTH ROMAN ODE

It will perhaps have been observed that the monumentality of the first four Roman Odes functions in varying ways, with no single ode presenting a single type of serious concern. Thus the first Roman Ode aspires to monumentality through display of the power of Jupiter, but concludes with various pictures of social response to the choices of values afforded in life. The second Roman Ode concentrates at its outset largely on these social pictures, but concludes with a re-assertion of the rewards of *virtus* and of God's power over the world regardless of its guilt or innocence. The third Roman Ode, by means of a lengthy historical exemplum in the form of a speech of Juno, links the themes of purposeful pursuit of *virtus*, Rome's greatness and the conditions on which the power of the state rests. The fourth Roman Ode presents again God's central power quelling disorder but mediates this vision through an assertion of the power of poetry, both in general and in specific reference to Horace himself. The social life briefly lost to sight in III.4 resurfaces in III.5, which, like III.6, examines the values and impelling motives in civic and private life: III.5 in terms of the historical past foreseeing the present, and III.6 in terms of the poet addressing the present and forecasting the future while contrasting it with the past. [1]

Thus as the Roman Odes move toward their final two segments, their audience's attention is increasingly addressed to an awareness of the present day. But this awareness has been shaped by the order of experience just briefly sketched; or, seen under a different aspect: the order of heaven and society (III.1), the categories of civic life in war and peace (III.2), Rome's credentials for success (III.3), and the power of art to further reflection and to canalize force (III.4). The final two poems of the cycle go on to present their vision of Roman potentiality and actuality in context: moral choice is fraught with civic consequence, and the individual citizen (Regulus in III.5, you Roman in III.6) is the setting for struggles and decisions that have grave implications for the state as well as for himself; the fabric of society, the order under heaven, can be fatally compromised and flawed by individual wrong-doing. In these two odes

---

[1] See also Eduard Fraenkel, *Horace* (Oxford: Oxford University Press, 1957), pp. 272ff., Steele Commager, *The Odes of Horace* (New Haven: Yale University Press, 1962), pp. 111f., and J. Krókowski, "Die Regulus-Ode des Horaz," *Eos* 56 (1966; actually 1969), pp. 151-160, on Cicero's influence in the poem.

the poet moves from presenting monumental statements with locutionary force to statements that are basically constative in their force.[2] But that force is, I repeat, carried out in the context created by the four preceding odes.

Though the figure of Regulus addressing the Senate is a monumental subject, the fifth Roman Ode nevertheless contrasts what has come before it in the monumental sequence of texts that we call the Roman Odes. Perhaps for that reason it is useful to begin detailed examination of the Regulus ode with its most apparent verbal similarity to the preceding ode: III.5.45f., *consilio dato,* and III.4.41f., *consilium et datis et dato gaudetis.* Both the fourth and fifth odes offer *consilium,* the one rooted in the historic present with Augustus, the other in Rome's distant past, with Regulus. The fourth and fifth ode are further related in that both have *caelo* in their opening lines. In III.4, the Muse is invited to come down from heaven to aid the poet. In III.5 heaven is the place where Jupiter rules at present and where Augustus, after certain events have taken place, will also be located. The *consilium* of the Muses in III.4 has its political side; the *consilium* of Regulus sharpens that political focus. Heaven, the final goal of Augustus' labors on earth, both makes the *consilium* available to the poet, and hence to us, in III.4, and provides the overarching framework that will validate and authenticate Augustus' political work, the modern-day working-out of Regulus' *consilium* to long-ago Rome. Thus the themes of III.4 and III.5, broadly conceived, are interlaced on the level of repetition of words embodying those themes.

More than elsewhere in the Roman Odes, Roman history is the context for this utterance's fuller comprehension. As Greek poets had done, so Horace likens Augustus' rule on earth to God's rule in heaven.[3] The first strophe's second pair of lines, "adiectis Britannis / imperio gravibus-que Persis," add a qualification that must be interpreted in light of the historical context. Julius Ceasar had landed in Britain in 55/4 B.C., but this tentative beginning, ending in failure, was not followed up, even

---

[2] For a discussion of these terms see J. L. Austin, *How to do Things with Words*[2] (Cambridge: Harvard University Press, 1975), pp. 99-109, and pp. 133-150, and passim. Cf. Stanley Fish, "How to do Things With Austin and Searle: Speech Act Theory and Literary Criticism," *Modern Language Notes* 91 (1976), pp. 983-1025.

[3] See Gordon Williams, *The Third Book of Horace's Odes* (Oxford: Oxford University Press, 1969), p. 59, and also *ad loc.* for the historical background; cf. Horace *Odes* I.12.49-60. For Horace's praise of Augustus, see E. Doblhofer, *Die Augustuspanegyrik des Horaz in formalhistorischer Sicht* (Heidelberg, 1966). For Augustus as vice-regent of God, see H. Haffner, "Die fünfte Römerode des Horaz," *Philologus* 93 (1938), pp. 132-156. It is the contention of V. Pöschl, *Entretiens Fondation Hardt II* (Genève, 1953), pp. 110f., 126, that the *Roman Odes* contain implied warnings for Augustus, as well as praise. See also his *Horaz und die Politik* (*Sitzungsberichte der Heidelberger Akademie der Wissenschaften,* Heidelberg, 1956).

though there is reason to believe Augustus early in his reign contemplated action against Britain. As for the Parthians (*Persis*, III.5.4) the defeat of Crassus at Carrhae in 53 B.C. is paramount in Roman-Persian relations.[4] Plans were afoot no doubt for a long time before the peace of 20 B.C. was contracted. This peace, represented as a victory for Rome, finally brought the return of Crassus' standards. One may confidently surmise that Horace addresses the capture of M. Atilius Regulus and five hundred Romans by the Carthaginians in 255 B.C. in light of these contemporary movements in working things out with Parthia. The Romans must not forget what Crassus lost, and the exemplum of Regulus provides the necessary warning. Augustus' divine credentials will be completed by the successful resolving of Rome's East-West foreign policies. The reference to Britain may be poetic rather than political in its prescriptive force. But the references to Crassus, exemplified by Regulus' speech, speak directly to contemporary foreign entanglements, the details of which the critic should possess.

This grounding of the next-to-last Roman Ode in contemporary outlook serves to root the whole series in a pragmatic function: to direct the awareness of the citizens, that is, the state's components, along certain moral lines. Having Regulus in mind provides the best framework in which to view relations with Parthia. Thus both poetry and history make impact on actual life. But the fifth Roman Ode is much more than a political tract, advocating one side of the argument that ensued when Augustus closed the temple of Janus in 29 B.C. and precipitated outcries from some for ransoming Rome's prisoners in Parthia. Rather the ode is clearly linked as well to the moral calculus set up by the whole series. The Roman soldiers captured by the Parthians (or Carthaginians, in the vocabulary of the Regulus speech) are in cold fact Romans no longer.[5] The Roman citizens enthralled by vice, ambition, and the other private defects that become public diseases in the Roman Odes are likewise true Romans no longer. The state's resources, Regulus says, would be badly used to ransom men enervated by living as captives, and the words he uses, *auro repensus*, recall the wrong use of private resources alluded to in III.1, e.g., 21ff., III.2, e.g., 1ff., III.3, 21f. (though this last might also be construed as civic funds witheld for personal gain), III.3.49ff., and by implication the virtue of slender means, III.4.9ff. Evidently the theme of greed is widely distributed through the cycle. Further, like III.2, III.3 and III.4 in part, III.5 represents the crossing of domestic boundaries

---

[4] See H. Fugier, "Horace et les Parthes," *Bulletin de la Faculté des Lettres de Strasbourg* 46 (1967), pp. 283-291.

[5] See G. Williams, *op. cit. supra*, n. 3, *ad loc.* for a discussion of *minor capitis* as *deminutio capitis*, implying loss of civil rights.

into foreign territories in military activities which are ideally successful in the case of the Roman warrior in III.2, made conditional by Juno in III.3.57ff., and both tinged with reminiscences of the civil war in III.4 37ff. and redolent with destructiveness, e.g., III.4.65ff.: "vis consili expers mole ruit sua." This use of *consilium* is significant in light both of Regulus' *consilium* in III.5.44, and that of the Muses in III.4.41 as analysis earlier noted. The theme of military thrust into foreign lands is closely identified with the theme of *consilium*, or the justification for each such action.

Let us in detail examine the Regulus ode in light of these tentative linkages with other poems in the cycle as experienced by a reader who has read the Roman Odes up to the fifth. The first strophe crosses two categories implemented over and over in the cycle: the past and the future, which bracket a present time out of which the poet speaks to a present audience. The thundering of Jupiter is a sign of war or peace, both portent and judgment, characterizing the age-old belief in the weather god, the sky-father Jupiter.[6] Belief in Augustus as a god among us on earth (the function of *praesens*) will similarly be characterized by an outward sign, the subjugation of Britain and Parthia to his rule. In graphic terms, god and ruler are symmetrical on the same plane: a feature also noted in contemporary Roman historical reliefs.[7] Thus this poem begins[8] with an assertion facing back to the rule of law and order in heaven of Ode III.4 and forward to its human corollary on earth, Rome's *imperium* exerted over her enemies, just as menacing as the giants were to Jupiter. Augustus has to be sure declared peace, and the Britains and Parthians cannot be added to the empire without further war. But characteristically Horace turns from the level of logic to the level of poetic image: Crassus' soldiers' degradation is presented in the second strophe in terms of family alliance with the enemy, and in the third strophe in terms of obliteration of Rome's sacred civic symbols such as the Salian shields that came down from heaven to Numa, and the *nomen Romanum*, the toga and Vesta's fire. The God thundering in heaven at the opening of strophe one is precisely the god enthroned in his Capitoline temple,

---

[6] This seems to be the implication of the pluperfect *credidimus*. Portents of thunder occurring through the year and often predicting concord or civil war were interpreted in the divinatory calendar *Tonitruale* of Nigidius Figulus, a contemporary of Cicero; see Kroll, *R-E.* 17, 208 f., and S. Weinstock, *Divus Julius* (Oxford: Oxford University Press, 1971), pp. 263f. The association in *Odes* III.5 of thunder and war is thus not accidental or fanciful; cf. *Odes* I.34.5-7.

[7] Though not contemporary with Horace, the Cancelleria Reliefs follow very closely the style of the *Ara Pacis Augustae*, and show the Emperor (Domitian) on the same plane as divine and divinized figures.

[8] We understand always the proviso that the cycle could be read as some MSS suggest, as a whole. See above, note 7, p. 7.

recollected through line twelve, "incolumi Iove et urbe Roma," an adaptation of the ancient sacral formula *salva urbe atque arce*.[9]

Regulus, incarnating values of ancient Rome, is introduced as an ancient exemplum in stark contrast to the modern Marsian and Apulian, whose geographic remoteness of origin one would willingly have thought guaranteed their pristine morals. Regulus, a figure from the past,[10] foresees for us now the *pernicies*, the rot, that comes "si non periret captiva pubes." The state must cut off those that have not lived up to the state's expectations of them. Those who join the enemy, be they Carthaginians of mid third century B.C. or Parthians of modern day (or even, perhaps, those opposing Augustus?) become the enemy and lose their Roman identity. The good of the institution of the state takes precedence over the well-being of those of its members who have trafficked with the enemy. Regulus' speech, inasmuch as it is the act of an individual equipped (unlike Juno in III.3) with such human characteristics as a wife, children, and a domestic career (as lines forty-one through fifty-six emphasize) softens the potential harshness of such a message by allowing us to see how disastrously this outlook affects one man, the speaker. He is destroyed, indeed precipitates his own destruction, by fully implementing the civic values which he espouses, but his exemplum is fully integrated into the history of the institution: both the state and this poetic exaltation of the state celebrate him.

Accordingly, the speech of Regulus as reported by Horace does not represent a rhetorical act directed at the senators who were wavering in their deliberations of how to handle their hostage problem.[11] His speech is not rhetorical but rather a series of aphorisms that ensue after his abrupt mid-strophe initiating of his speech with vivid eye-witness reportage: "vidi, vidi," line twenty-one. Further, Regulus' speech to the Roman Senate is the only other directly reported speech act in the cycle besides Juno's speech to the heavenly assembly in III.3. As Juno sets down divine sanctions on Rome's historical progress, based on outward actions and moral presumptions, so too Regulus' discourse puts limits on Roman greatness should certain moral precepts not be followed. Like Juno, (III.3.49, *aurum inrepertum*) Regulus mentions gold, *auro repensus*, III.5.25,[12] as the symbol of moral defect, and he also invokes *vera virtus* in

[9] G. Williams, *op. cit. supra*, n. 3, p. 58, n. 1.

[10] Comparison has been made to Odysseus: L. Hinckley, "Regulus and Odysseus," *Classical Bulletin* 55 (1979), pp. 56-58.

[11] So George Kennedy, *The Art of Rhetoric in the Roman World* (Princeton: Princeton University Press, 1972), p. 399.

[12] Note that both locales exhibit the prefix *re-* immediately after the metal is mentioned, and involve verbs in *pe-*: *reperio* and *rependo*.

line twenty-nine in a context of civic responsibility exercised in foreign wars, much like *virtus'* context in III.2.17ff. and 21ff. Regulus further asserts that fear of death and loss of civic identity and disregard of the state's values came about through dependence on one's enemy through long captivity: a set of actions forestalled in the second Roman Ode by the assertion "dulce et decorum est pro patria mori," III.2.13.

Regulus concludes his fictive speech (the fictiveness of which Horace emphasizes in these ways) by asserting that the captive, uprooted and deranged, confuses peace with war, and no longer knows the way to win his life: a theme voiced at the very outset of the cycle in the confusion of moral values set forth in III.1. Thus major elements in his words can be linked both thematically and verbally to other leading ideas in other poems in this cycle. The poems resonate in different registers and contexts a relatively narrow range of themes, just as a large and complex historical relief often keeps to relatively few statements.

Four and a half strophes precede Regulus' discourse, wherein Horace mediates between present and past. Four strophes succeed the speech, wherein Horace lingers on the private, human dimension of Regulus' situation, and does not return us in time to the present, but rather foreshadows only Regulus' immediate unpleasant prospects. The four final strophes are divided in half by the strong particle *atqui,* line forty-nine, which accompanies a change of tense, the imperfect indicative *sciebat.* Before *atqui,* Horace has allowed the verb *fertur,* line forty-one, to dominate the two preceding strophes: "They say he put from himself the kiss of his chaste wife and his little children..." This *fertur* achieves distance from the immediately preceding presentation of Regulus, and gains a historical dimension as well. Regulus has, in *vidi, vidi,* line thirty-one, functioned as an eyewitness. Now he too has his witness. The narrative reasserts itself as the compelling picture of Regulus and his civic and domestic situation is reviewed. His *consilium* to the Roman Senate can now be characterized as *numquam alias datum,* line forty-six. But in what context? Solely that of advice hitherto given to the *patres conscripti* in the history of Rome. The implications of Regulus' *consilium,* its inner values and moral premises, and of course this present mediation of his famous dictum are all made available through the Roman Odes. The *consilium* of the Muses and of Juno have been interwoven with the moral and hence historical fabric of Rome from her inception in Troy. By drawing attention in III.5.45ff. to the temporal dimension Horace directs the audience to the human, immediate quality of the event he has just recalled for them. But by using the word *consilium* he insures that the attentive reader will integrate this historical exemplum into the continuity of artistic event that the cycle has hitherto made available to him.

The second half of the ode's concluding movement concentrates on the reverberations of the scene of dramatic farewell just presented. If the poet makes his intervening art noticeable in the phrase *consilium numquam alias datum,* he likewise makes himself apparent in the *atqui* sentence, which changes the tone from one of reportage (*fertur*) to commentary: the poet tells us what was going on in Regulus' mind, and contrasts it with his outer actions. "And yet he knew what the barbarian torturer was readying for him…" Regulus goes to his fate as if he were going to a country holiday after a long Roman day of litigation had finally ended and a judgment for a client had been pronounced. The poet emphasizes the every-day setting of Regulus' extraordinary action and characterizes in these every-day terms Regulus' deportment in order to provide access to the *consilium* on an every-day level, graspable by any reader. One may not be familiar with the god, Muses or *princeps,* but one had a sense of what a Roman business day was.[13] Further, by returning the ode to this level of domestic reality, Horace creates the opportunity for seeing that the enemy we might be accused of consorting with, the enemy that renders us oblivious of our Roman worth, might exist in a domestic setting as well as beyond the empire's frontiers, or in lyric poems: a theme to be carefully explored in the sixth and final Roman Ode, but foreshadowed by this choice of ending for the fifth. The practically mythic stature of Regulus, underscored by the use of *fertur,* line forty-one, makes his story available on more than the historical level; the moral dimensions are unmistakable, and more on the surface than with much ancient historiography. The explicit exemplum of line fifteen would be the wrongheaded decision to ransom Regulus and his five hundred companions; the *pernicies* of line sixteen covers both a shameful treating with Parthia for the standards and remnants of Crassus' army, and the moral degradation which that would imply.[14] But it likewise extends to the realm of personal morality in every-day life (a theme Horace explores in *Satires* and *Epistles* as well), through the application of the principle of reading the whole cycle as a recurring and stable projection of vocabulary making statements on dif-

---

[13] This also has a bearing on the domestic emphasis in III.6, as we will see. The vocabulary of the *Odes* in general, as of the *Aeneid,* tends somewhat toward everyday language; see L. P. Wilkinson, "The Language of Vergil and Horace," *Classical Quarterly* 9 (1959), pp. 181-192.

[14] The image of the dyed wool not regaining its former color or purity seems to be associated with moral discussions: Persius 3.37 and the scholium: "metaphora a lana, quae corrupta ad pristinum colorem reverti non potest." Ennius' comment along the same lines, probably in protest against the ransoming of Roman prisoners taken at Cannae, is also pertinent in connection with Horace's passage: "cum illud quo iam semel est imbuta veneno," *Ann.* 5.35. The image, like so many others in the Roman Odes, is an old one, and operates often in a moral context.

ferent levels of meaning and hence capable of a wide, but not a boundless, range of interpretation.

An examination of how Horace manipulates the end of III.5 along these lines may be useful. The *egregius exul,* line forty-eight, electing not to return to Rome again out of free choice, and hence noble, departs from a setting of his civic labors that is as detailed and as programmatic as any historical relief. The Senate has met in the Curia, and Regulus, moving through the crowd outside it, makes his way past the sculpture of Marsyas, between the Comitium and the Lacus Curtius, where the *lites* (line fifty-four), the law cases, were held. The rôle he exhibits is that of a *patronus* who has looked after his client's time-consuming case and is leaving town after the verdict; note that we are not told which way it went. Regulus has done his civic duty regardless of outcome, whether he and his client have won or lost: a duty extraordinary on the level of the actual choice he made, to return to certain and painful death in Carthage, but mundane and every-day on the level of the picture which the poet's words transmit. The very strong contrast between outer aspect and inner significance is reinforced by having Regulus' calm departure have as its hypothetical destination, in accord with his deliberate withdrawing, the territory of Venafrum, well-known for its fine olive oil, or Tarentum, famous for both oil and honey, and both elegant places for relaxation in a country villa, and both very unlike Carthage. These place names unmistakably imply an encomium of landscape associated with the world of the pastoral. The reference to "Lacedomonian Tarentum" is interesting; could Horace be referring to Pindar *Olympian* 18 wherein Phalanthus the Laconian leader is praised as that city's founder?[15] If so, Horace as celebrant of its latter-day non-arriving visitor links himself to Pindar once again.

For Regulus, the case is over, *diiudicata lite,* and the verdict in. So too was it for Horace, and for everyone who would read his poems. The lines of duty ran clear, from Regulus through the centuries to the present day. It remains for the sixth Roman Ode to show how awareness of responsibility does not insure right action.

---

[15] Tarentum and Venafrum figure also in *Odes* II.6.11ff; see also E. Paratore, "Taranto nella poesia augustea," *Rassegna Pugliese* I.2 (1966), pp. 1-24.

CHAPTER EIGHT

THE SIXTH ROMAN ODE

If *carmen* III.5, in its pictures of Regulus addressing the Roman senate and taking leave of his family and friends in the Forum comes closest of the Roman Odes to a Roman historical relief, and hence to plastic art in general, in its assignable locale, the final ode makes only slight reference to real architectural monumentality, and interestingly enough does this at its outset: the temples and shrines of the gods, their neglect, and their potential renovation. The balance of the ode, whilst abounding in vivid pictures, as will be noted, mediates a moral calculus that cannot be embodied in pictorial art. By stressing the primacy of poetry in this way at the end of the cycle, Horace again emphasizes the power of his art, and by implication his stature as a poet and as seer.

The text in twelve strophes can be divided for purposes of elucidating its progression and its relations with the preceding poems into groups of four strophes.[1] The opening has very often been linked to Augustus' beginning, in 28 B.C., a program of restoring Roman temples and priesthoods that had fallen into neglect and desuetude,[2] and the original audience would have found itself in the midst of these projects, which finally encompassed the restoration of eighty-two temples in the City. But further, the *templa* in strophe one proceed naturally enough from the civic setting of Regulus' farewell in the Forum Romanum, probably to be imagined not far from the site of the new temple of Divus Iulius, near the Temple of Castor and Pollux, and dedicated in 29 B.C. In any event, the mention of the temples accords with the sacerdotal character of the strophe's opening words, pronouncing judgment (*inmeritus, donec*) on *Romanus*, you Roman citizen, caught up through accident of being born a descendent of sinful ancestors in their guilt. By the very Roman renewal of civic buildings the somewhat unroman guilt through inheritance or blood-line is to be atoned for, or so the *vates* asserts. The unqualified confidence of Horace's pronouncement on guilt, the gods and the state, met again in the final strophe of the text, recalls the sacral character of the very first strophe of the cycle, III.1.1-4, as well as the tone of pronouncement in the opening of the preceding ode, III.5.1-4, and the confidence of command issued in III.4.1-4: poems one, four, five and six begin with a

---

[1] See also the discussion of III.6 in Eduard Fraenkel, *Horace* (Oxford: Oxford University Press, 1957), pp. 261, 285ff.

[2] *Res Gestae* 20.4.

one-strophe sentence wherein the poet's sacral and moral authority is manifested and renewed, a recurring feature of the cycle gaining cumulative effect that crests in the final strophe of the sixth poem.

The poet's division of the final poem in the Roman Odes into three symmetrical parts likewise parallels a division of the only poem of the cycle in twelve strophes, the opening poem. There a division into three groups of four strophes each, including the opening four lines, is possible along thematic lines (strophes one through four: order and class; five through eight: dissatisfaction and contentment; nine through twelve: ambition's limitations) but there the breaking points, though quite apparent through the contrasting pictures beginning in strophes five and nine, do not serve a progression of ideas as do those in III.6: strophes one through four: the state and its dangers; five through eight: domestic corruption; nine through twelve: domestic virtues of the past as benefits of the state; gnome of present decay, both social and civic. Nevertheless, the identical number of strophes, including the first two being end-stopped, and the tripartite division, strongly suggest that Odes III.1 and III.6 were made to look somewhat alike in their functioning as introductory and concluding texts for the sequence.[3]

To return to III.6 itself: the second strophe, in its adumbration of the chain of command, "dis te minorem, quod geris, imperas," likewise looks back to the second strophe of III.1, with its hierarchy of God, kings and ruled peoples. Further, the second strophe of III.6 encapsulates other elements from elsewhere in the Roman Odes; for instance, *di neglecti*, III.6.7, recalls *Diespiter neglectus* of III.2.29f. (its concluding strophe), and the attentive reader will soon discover further parallels, both lexical and other, such as correspondence between theme and strophe length, word placement, etc., between the first phases of the final poem in the series and its antecedents. For instance, the sixth line of the poem, "hinc [viz., the gods] omne principium, huc refer exitum," has,

---

[3] Nothing is implied about the simultaneity of composition of III.1 and III.6, although obviously the question can be raised. Both poems also touch on religious matters, e.g., 'sacerdos Musarum,' III.1.3, and 'di neglecti,' III.6.7. For the religious context, we should bear in mind that the connection between the *di neglecti* and the state's potential faltering was well-established. Cicero had made many suggestions about religious reforms in *De re publica* and later in his *De legibus*. Around 47 B.C. Varro published his *Antiquitates rerum divinarum*, dedicated to Julius Caesar as Pontifex Maximus. Its purpose was to save the gods from perishing through negligence of the Romans; Varro asserted that the Romans conquered the world because of their piety toward the gods, and implied that the Empire would survive if the gods received their due; (Frag. 36 Ag., Tertullian *Apol.* 25; cf. Minucius Felix 25.1 and S. Weinstock, *Divus Julius* (Oxford: Oxford University Press, 1971), p. 181; M. P. Charlesworth, "Pietas and Victoria," *Journal of Roman Studies* 33 (1943), pp. 1-10. On Horace's probable ideology as *vates*, see F. Solmsen, "Die Dichteridee des Horaz und ihre Probleme," *Zeitschrift für Aesthetik* 26 (1932), pp. 160ff.

in the context of line five, *imperas,* a military connotation. Juno's speech
in the third Roman Ode, III.3.49ff., speaks of how the Romans come to
world domination, and imputes military success to healthy fear of and
respect for the gods. Her context is attitude toward gold as the index to
moral superiority: a point not without bearing for the cycle's concluding
poem as well. Further, the sixth poem's third strophe, with its reference
to the Roman expedition of Oppius Statianus against Parthia's general
Monaeses resonates the picture of a Roman campaign to foreign parts in
III.2.6ff., and contrasts to its presumed success Oppius' loss of two
legions of Antony's army at the hands of the Parthians in 36 B.C. and the
defeat in 40 B.C. of the army of the Syrian legate L. Decidius Saxa by
Pacorus, who interestingly enough is the son of the king of Parthia, a
shadowy reminiscence perhaps of the *regius sponsus* of III.2.10.

The defeats,[4] the poet avers, were inflicted on campaigns that were *inauspicatos impetus,* III.6.10.[5] The technical term deserves comment. Since
not once but twice Roman forces moving against Parthia were defeated,
and since the assistance of the divinity is assured by valid auspices, each
military operation must have been commenced *non auspicato,* the *di neglecti*
withholding their aid. The twofold failure of course makes the divine
displeasure even more unmistakable. Horace, as *sacerdos* and as *vates,*
positions taken principally in III.1.1-4 and III.4.5ff., namely the beginning and middle of the Roman Odes, here appears as judge of what sin
the present age incurs because of its forebears, and, more particularly
pronounces what was not (and by implication what is) favored by the
gods through auspices. The urban project of rebuilding temples would
have been accompanied by taking the auspices, and this favored enterprise will offset the guilt characterized by the unfavored external military
projects of war against Parthia, and, in the fourth strophe, the nearly
unsuccessful defense of the Rumanian border from the Dacians and the
City Rome itself from "Aethiops," the Egyptians, here presented not as
participants in Antony's civil war against Rome, but as a foreign
antagonist. Rome, distracted by civil disorder, nearly falls prey to foreign
attack. These near successes of Rome's enemies reveal the enmity of
heaven, and immediately there come to mind the provisos of Juno's

---

[4] Note that *bis,* "twice," stands early in the sentence and is thus emphasized.

[5] On-the-spot auguries for engaging the enemy in battle, *auspicia ex tripudiis,* may be
what Horace has in mind in III.6.10, *inauspicatos impetus,* but he likely as well meant
auspicia publica undertaken in connection with the armies in question setting out from
Rome. Unlike dependence on the *tripudium sollistimum,* the *auspicia publica* would involve
caelestia auspicia and *signa ex avibus,* as would temple re-dedications; the former is thus
probably a significant aspect of the preceding poem's opening, *Caelo tonantem Iovem,*
III.5.1ff., a sign likewise linked to Rome's conquering of her enemies.

address in III. 3.37ff., where in quick succession both Parthia (line forty-four) and Egypt (line forty-eight) are found, characterizing Roman rule.

Thus the first four strophes of III.6 show, on the negative side, the crimes of the present generation's ancestors (*Delicta maiorum*, line one), the disrepair and neglect of the City's temples and cult statues (*aedes labentes deorum et foeda nigro simulacra fumo*) and hence of Rome's gods, the precedent of divine attack on Hesperia because of human neglect of cult (*di multa neglecti dederunt Hesperiae mala luctuosae*), the two Eastern defeats, and the Dacian and Egyptian threats. On the positive side is found only the verb *imperas* (line five) and its explanation, *dis te minorem quod geris* (ibid.) The imperative command, to refer and ascribe every beginning and ending to the gods, (line six), and the clause *donec refeceris,* and what follows (line two) are also positive in tone, but evidently do not characterize the present state of Rome or its citizens. This negative if not gloomy picture of Rome at home and abroad is accounted for by the second segment of the poem, strophes five through eight.

If the first segment links the gods to the state through the transgressions of the present citizen's forebears and his contemporary measures for atonement, the second segment centers on the citizen's private life and its taints. The *disciplina domestica* is tainted by corruption, and has been for some time. The poet contrives a rather ponderous sentence to express this: "Generations [*saecula*] teeming with sin first tainted marriages and the racial stock and home." Why *saecula*? The word implies a perspective on time that goes back into the past, and basically means first a lifespan and then "generation." The flawed family is regarded as a poisoned source or spring bringing consequent corruption to the larger institutions of the *patria*, the state as a large family (with its *parens*, Augustus) and the *populus*, what one is tempted to call the gene pool. The poet declines to be specific as to the time of this deterioration's beginning, though he makes plain, by his use of the perfect tense, *fluxit*, line twenty, that deleterious effects have spread far and wide already.

We may note that Horace has spoken in the first strophe of this second section of the ode (lines seventeen through twenty) in rather general terms. The second, third and fourth strophes that make up this central panel are vivid with detail. We pass from the world of civic cult and military threat of the ode's first section, epic in theme and tone, to the private world of elegy that dominates the second section after its first strophe, the generalities of which match the elevated tone of the first section. The world inhabited by the *matrona virgo*, a girl unmarried but of marriageable age, is one she characterizes by her delight in learning risqué dances and the arts of providing pleasure. Her personality is further suggested by the economic *iam nunc* of line twenty-three: even now, in her unmarried state, she dwells wholeheartedly on extra-marital lovers. Between strophes, as it were, she gets married and we next see her in section two's third strophe "soon" (*mox,* line twenty-five) seeking out younger lovers at dinner parties given with her husband: a succinct touch characterizing his nature as well as hers, carried further in the section's fourth strophe: he connives at her extra-marital adventures, trade-off possibly for some unspeakable activity of his own. This woman, straight from the world of an Ovid, a Tibullus or a Propertius, is given a psychological dimension fully as developed as the figures in elegy. She does not view her partners as men individualized in some way; she invokes no personal likes but rather is completely indiscriminate as well as completely loose: a moral defect of considerable proportions even by elegy's standards.[6]

Horace takes only three strophes to present this woman moving from unmarried young adulthood when she is obsessed by erotic preoccupations to marriage when she lures lovers younger than herself in leisurely and open fashion at her husband's parties, and also leaves the house when invited to give herself to now a business man, now a Spanish ship captain who pays lavishly for her favors.[7] Her world is that of elegy, but its seamy side, its degradation of matronal responsibility; the woman is not an elegiac figure in that her husband is not the jealous mate to be outwitted by the stratagems of elegy and in that she herself has no emotional involvement with her swiftly changing partners. The picture, though small in scale, is one of incisive portrayal of a situation deeply corrupt, and totally outside the structure and conventions of erotic elegy as a literary form. As a picture, however, of the social side effects of trying to make a literary genre into a style of life, it resonates the recurring forms of elegy, such as dancing, the other *artes, amores,* young lovers, the husband, parties, the lights turned low, and assignations. But it yokes these conventions to an ethical, not a literary framework, just as the epic elements of the ode's first section, strophes one through four, are put in service of the ethos of the state and its survival.

Just as the master image of national or racial line flawed by sin dominates the opening of the poem, and serves as bridge to its second section, at the beginning of which (lines seventeen following) the *saecula* implied by the *maiores* and the *Romanus* of the present day (lines one and

---

[6] Cf. Catullus 68.140, where Jupiter is characterized as *omnivolus.* On the curious expression in line 24, *de tenero ungui,* see A. Cameron, "Tener ungui," *Classical Quarterly* 15 (1965), pp. 80-83. It has been suggested that Propertius' elegies imitated the *Roman Odes*; see W. R. Nethercut, "The Ironic Priest: Propertius' Roman Elegies, III.1-5: Imitations of Horace and Vergil," *American Journal of Philology* 91 (1970), pp. 385-407.

[7] Senatorial bias against trade, and general Roman bias against foreigners can be seen here.

two) are said to be carriers of guilt, *culpa* (line seventeen), so too this image of generation and of descent of stock forms the transition from the second to the third and final section of four strophes, lines thirty-three and following: "youth sprung from parents such as these did not tinge the billows with Punic blood..." Horace leaves in the dark just who the *parentes* are: the degenerate woman and her husband, or the woman and one of her lovers. At any rate the term *parens*, with connotations of reverence for ancestors in the festival of the Parentalia, hardly has more than biological significance here. A child from such a household is doomed no matter who the father be. The vivid contrast between this epigone and the soldiers who vanquished Carthage in the first Punic War, annihilated Pyrrhus and felled Antiochus and Hannibal the terrible, is achieved economically by presenting in this final section's second strophe the social context of these brave men: virile progeny of country fighters, accustomed to hard agricultural work. Their mother is a *mater severa* who bids them bring home firewood. The picture of rural life, wherein repose the values of the past, and whose very *rusticitas*, pilloried by elegy, is the secret source of Rome's possible strength, is somewhat softened in the third strophe, lines forty-one through forty-four. Here in the third section pastoral imagery succeeds the epic and elegiac tones of the first and second movements of this ode: "when Sun was varying the shadows on the mountains, and was removing the yokes from the tired oxen, bringing back the friendly evening-tide in his departing car." The Regulus Ode, III.5, ends on a pastoral note too, with the associations of oil and pleasant landscape of Venafrum and Tarentum, but in III.6 we are closer to Rome, in fact in Sabine territory (*Sabellis ligonibus,* line thirty-eight) and the picture is quite close to those at the end of Vergil's first, sixth and tenth eclogues.[8]

The first three strophes of this poem's conclusions consist of one long sentence, moving from the contrast between effete society and antique Roman valor to that valor's country roots and ancient values, to a pastoral picture of the end of a country day's labor: a picture seemingly gratuitous as far as developing the line of thought is concerned. The epic coloring of strophes one through four, and the elegiac precipitate in strophes five through eight, have a teaching and enhancing function. The pastoral coloring in strophes ten and eleven serves to remind us that another world exists, the source of Rome's earlier greatness. But like

---

[8] E.g., Vergil, *Ecl.* X.83: "maioresque cadunt altis de montibus umbrae." Juvenal also used these Vergilian pictures for contrast: see the present writer's "Juvenal III: an eclogue for the Urban Poor," *Hermes* 90 (1962), pp.244-248. See also B. Fenik, "Horace's First and Sixth Roman Ode and the Second Georgic," *Hermes* 90 (1962), pp. 72-96, especially pp. 90ff.

Regulus in III.5 we cannot go there. We must instead direct our attention to what follows the long, soaring lyric sentence of strophes nine, ten
and eleven: the terse, two-sentence conclusion to the sixth Roman Ode
and to the whole cycle: the gnome of time the destroyer, time conceived
of along the lines of the ode's master image: generation succeeded by
generation, the later weaker and less moral than the earlier. Time's
passage brings ruin to the temples' outward fabric. Time's passage
brings decay to Rome's social fabric as well by vitiating the inner moral
fibre of her citizens. This too, like the temples, can be rebuilt and
restored to good condition. Horace makes this suggestion only obliquely,
by means of the organization of the poem, not by means of an open statement. Literature's conventions, its vocabulary, its drive for unity in this
poem's symmetry of sections, is invoked to make the final point of the
cycle: use time well, rebuild in time. On the level of message, the poem
concludes in pessimism; how different would it be if the last strophe could
be suppressed! On the level of literary art, the competent reader may
recuperate the optimism of the poem's opening, the value of taking the
action of rebuilding the temples of the gods, and impute it to the poem's
conclusion: veneration of the gods must be accompanied by inner moral
revitalization, the necessity for which must be hammered home. We
must not think things cannot get worse. We are locked into a genera-
tional pattern of decay; just as neglected architecture undergoes
deterioration through time, so did we and so do we now. Intervention is
essential to reverse the process, and the function of the final strophe, so
vividly presenting its gnome of decay, is to shake us into this awareness.
What we do with this insight is extra-literary, whether we wrap ourselves
in the inevitability of the maxim the poet delivers as the text's conclusion
or whether we involve ourselves in the whole poem and its less than
pessimistic opening. The literary world moves on to III.7, "Quid fles,
Asterie," to the world of young lovers with Greek names delicately
examining the psychological processes of memory, absence and potential
infidelity: a subject hardly consonant with the grim picture at the end of
III.6, or following out its moral implications. Horace by following the
cycle with a poem like III.7 underscores what literature is: not life, not
doctrine, not ethics after all, though sometimes civically monumental,
like the Roman Odes, sometimes slight, like "Quid fles, Asterie," whose
pair of lovers do not live in Rome, but in literature.

    Horace has used the category of the first person plural only once in the
Roman Odes before the *nos* of III.6.47, and that is the *credidimus* of
III.5.1, where both person and tense emphasize the antiquity and
ubiquity of belief in the thundering sky-father, soon to be joined as a god
by Augustus. The poet at the end of the cycle involves his audience and

also himself in one category, the present undifferentiated generation. That self that is linked to all who inherit guilt is as well the close associate of the Muses in III.4, and is there characterized as safe from harm. Further, the self at the end of the cycle is the self that rejects ambition at the end of III.1.45ff., and shuns the oath-breaker at the end of III.2.26ff., and directs his Muse to leave off epic recital and to conform to generic convention at the end of III.3.69ff., and who joins the believers in God's power in heaven at the beginning of III.5. Thus Horace in each of the poems has established a place for himself to appear in one way or another. Only one of these appearances is authorial, that is, as poet per se, and that is at the end of III.3. In the other places the persona of the poet engages the theme, not the act of poetic locution. In the two places where the first person plural subsumes the poet into a large group, it is into a mass incapable of being individualized or of willing themselves out of the group: the Indo-Europeans who have from time immemorial believed in the sky-father, (III.5.1) and *nos nequiores*, all who happen to constitute the present generation (III.6.47).

The poet who has the credentials to pronounce judgment (or sentence) on "you Roman" in III.6.1ff., has been authenticated during the cycle, especially in III.1.1-4, as enjoying this right or function by a privilege granted by the Muses. Art's privilege is to teach the state by addressing its components, *tu Romane* III.6.1ff., Augustus in III.4.37ff., and so forth. Art thus speaks through the mouth of one of us: *nos nequiores* can be impeded from bringing forth progeny more vicious than ourselves if the redeeming message of art is heeded.

The cycle of Roman Odes does not end in pessimism. Rather, the urgency of the cycle's monumental representation of past greatness, present vice and folly, and potential decrepitude or potential greatness is underlined by the desperate last strophe of III.6. To speak broadly, the one set of possibilities is adumbrated in III.5 and III.6, the other in III.1, 2, and 3. Ode III.4 pivots on *vis* and its dangers if uncontrolled by *consilium*. The vigor of law, national purpose and individual civic responsibility can be sapped by self-indulgence and softness on the level of the life of the individual citizen. Carthage as it were rises on the ruins of the individual corrupted Roman (cf. III.5.38ff.). By charging his observations with the urgency of the end of III.6 Horace elevates his cycle of odes from artistic event to civic exhortation on a monumental scale. By incorporating his priestly self into the mass of Roman citizenry slipping into deliquescence, he avoids the stance of the preacher who is preserved from the ills he castigates by his own special virtue. But more significantly, he makes his art, his function as *Musarum sacerdos*, inseparable from the problems his generation of Romans both face and constitute. Hence the prescribed audience of III.1.4: *virginibus puerisque canto.* By taking the six odes as a monumental unity we find the *progenies* of III.6.48 identifiable with the "new generation" whom the poet addressed as persons capable of heeding his warning, seeing his vision, hearing his song, and implementing a new foundation for the state.[9] This new direction seeks its exemplars from the Roman past, and its energy from the heavenly mandate that includes the divinity of Augustus.[10] The greatest dangers to it are apathy, avarice, ambition for self and not for the common welfare, inner disharmony and lack of *virtus,* blind force, and basely coming to terms with forces seeking Rome's ruin. The children of this, "our" generation, are bent to further this decline, but their awareness of its danger, through the artistic act of the Roman Odes, can sensitize them to resist it, change its direction by the *consilium* of the Muses, and further it with divine help into improvement not decadence.[11]

The first three odes, as suggested already, present the dangers in muted terms, their historical solutions in positive and traditional terms, e.g., III.1.25ff., III.2.13ff., III.3.1ff., 37ff., etc. The fourth ode is the turning point and appropriately centers on the poet's person, his sacrosanctity, his vision, and the heavenly paradigm of the forces of order containing (but just barely containing) the forces of chaos. When we come in Odes Five and Six to work out the heavenly pattern in the affairs of Rome, whose battle against chaos is not so definitively won, it may be thought, as is that of the gods against the giants,[12] we see in III.5 the moment when a single man, Regulus, using his insight into what would happen if the Senate ransomed his fellow soldiers from the Carthaginians, sways the state to a certain course of action. Regulus is obviously a type for Horace the poet likewise through his monumental composition counselling a given course of action. The Italian landscape is intact and its ancient peace professed as III.5 draws to its conclusion. But in III.6 it is not the third century B.C. any more, but contemporary Augustan

---

[9] Vergil's *Aeneid* can be seen as a foundation epic for the new state. See also Stefan Weinstock, *Divus Julius* (Oxford: Oxford University Press, 1971), pp. 175ff. for a good discussion of the idea's development. One may consider the Roman Odes as an artistic representation, analogous to a civic relief emphasizing foundation and new beginning in terms of old legends, like Aeneas and the White Sow on the *Ara Pacis Augustae.*

[10] For a wealth of contemporary detail on Augustus as a god, see S. Weinstock, *op. cit. supra,* n. 9, *s.v.* Augustus. In view of Horace's vocabulary in the Roman Odes, it is useful to recall that in 27 B.C. Augustus was awarded by the Senate and Roman people a golden shield, awarded for his *virtus, clementia, iustitia* and *pietas* "erga deos patriamque." It is probably over-ingenious to link this Clupeus Virtutis to Pallas' shield in III.4.57.

[11] Cf. III.4.65ff.

[12] Yet *nec peredit* (III.4.75) and what follows recalls *Furor Impius* at the end of Jupiter's speech in the first book of the *Aeneid* (I.294ff) which demon is not annihilated but similarly imprisoned, raising the possibility of future outbreak of his destructive forces like those of the giants.

Rome, with *Romane* receiving the full force of the poet's attention: the present generation who heeds not the *carmina* of III.1.2ff., and not the *virgines puerique* of III.1.4 whom the poet has hopes of rehabilitating before they undergo the genetic decline held up as a dreadful possibility, indeed certainty, at the end of III.6.45ff., "damnosa quid non inminuit dies?," if time's corrupting force is not mitigated.

The present generation is assigned a concrete task, the renovation of the gods' temples, and a reason for success: "dis te minorem quod geris, imperas," III.6.5. The recent past, not the romantic Republican past of III.2, and III.5, or the mythic past of III.3 and III.4, is set forth in III.6, culminating in a reference to the civil war (III.6.9-16). The immediate future is consequently painted in the darkest of terms in the Ode's second and third sections, as noted above. This pessimistic, even sociologically mordant picture of the corruption of a Roman household, and the great falling-off from the example of the past, and the bitter assertion of the final strophe, do not, because they come at the end, necessarily constitute Horace's final view of Rome's chances for regeneration and consequent success. We should notice that the final two strophes of the poem that ends the Roman Odes alternate between *now*, the depraved society of the *matura virgo*, and *then*, the strong morality of the past and its pastoral setting. The attractive picture from the genre of pastoral is shattered by the gnome from literature of morality, and we are returned to the present time, the dimension of time in which we view Horace's monument as its original audience. But the last panel but one, the tranquil end of a day of labor in the country, is not to be set aside as forgotten or obliterated through the force of the final assertion. The Vergilian image is what we must fight to regain, informed as we now are by Horace's vision of what we may do to shape nothing less than Rome's future.

Just as resolve to restore the ruined dwellings of the gods in the City reverses the effects of time, so too can the relentless deterioration of Roman virtue be arrested if Horace's call to moral re-armament is heeded. The last strophe of the Sixth Roman Ode is thus linked to the first strophe of the First Roman Ode. The *profanum volgus* of III.1.1 is the element that does not heed the poet's *carmina*, III.1.2ff., which *carmina* we who have read through the cycle now possess: the Roman Odes themselves. Viewed in this way, with III.6.45-48 and III.1.1-4 bound together as a self-implicating unit, the children of III.1.1ff. gain in meaning, and the *profanum volgus* in particularization. The poet as priest of the Muses is no less absent from the end of III.6 than elsewhere in the cycle. He asserts his gnomic statement, but through the process of reading the preceding six poems, with their precepts furthered by the Muses, a way out of the spiral of decline is afforded: it consists in re-examining the whole monumental sequence of Roman Odes in light of III.6.45-48, bearing in mind that one's actions and attitudes make one a part of the *profanum volgus* or not.

Further, by analogy with civic monuments such as the *Ara Pacis Augustae* one can infer that one "reading" of the text, or walk through the architectural structure, was not sufficient to sort out all the levels of implication raised by, in the case of a plastic monument, choice of site, orientation, order of reliefs as determined by entrance, etc. So too one must read and even more important re-read all of Book III of the *Odes* before the whole picture begins to be adumbrated: or better, before the notion of a "whole picture" can be formed.

With specific reference to the Roman Odes, the term cycle is important. The visitor to a site adorned with historical reliefs tends to end his inspection near the place where it began, and thus one is invited to re-examine the whole anew, or actually, to examine the monument with a newly acquired sense of its potential wholeness. Just so with the Roman Odes if the end of III.6 sends us back to the beginning of III.1 with greater insight into the nature of the *carmina* just experienced and the urgency of their themes. For *we*, the audience, find ourselves mirrored at the end of III.6. Just as "we" are engaged in re-ordering the temples (and other civic buildings as well)[13] so too "we" are inextricably involved in the processes of guilt and atonement such re-building is linked to by Horace in III.6.1ff. So too "we" must select ourselves as part of Horace's audience and become part of the group who heeds him, or part of the group which, hearing, ignores the import of his message. For the gods, Augustus and the Muses use his art to teach us.

Assigning a proleptic rôle to III.6.45-48 by suggesting it leads back to III.1.1-4 also results in making III.6 "end" on the note of peace in the rural fastness of Italy: again a theme to be met with in, say the *Ara Pacis Augustae*. But in Horace's total vision, not on the scale of III.6 but on the scale of the whole of the Roman Odes, Roman peace and tranquility is a part of, a necessary condition for, the *oikoumene* of world peace and prosperity. By suggesting through the deeply moving and very Vergilian picture in the next-to-last strophe of III.6 that the cycle could have ended thus, the poet impels us further to actualize that possibility. By making III.1.1-4 a kind of detachable preface to the whole cycle, as some critics have done,[14] one does no violence to the sequence as a whole, but rather one is enabled to see it in a larger perspective. Likewise, by making III.6.45-48 a kind of detachable epilogue attracted powerfully to

---

[13] The Regia in the Forum Romanum is a good example of Augustus' restorations. As seat of the *rex sacrorum*, it was associated with Divus Julius, and with state cult.

[14] *Supra*, pp. 6f.

III.1.1-4, one does no formal violence to III.6 (though of course the ordering of the text into three sections of four strophes each is compromised; yet there is a very abrupt break between III.6.44 and 45, more so in fact than between III.6.16 and 17). The cycle is allowed to repose at its near-ending on a note of deep domestic pastoral peace: a peace which we can have if we work to make Horace's promises come true.

EPILOGUE AND ODES III.7

The foregoing observations and interpretations concerning Horace's Roman Odes constitute a kind of fluid reading of this stable text in its fixed form mediating varied statements. Balance and perspective it is hoped have been maintained by keeping in mind that the poet teaches his audience to read his text and thus provides through the text limits and boundaries for valid interpretation. A few concluding remarks may be useful in assessing what lines of thought this particular act of classical criticism has followed.

We have obviously not exploited New Criticism and addressed III.1-6 as individual free-standing texts. Rather we have demonstrated that the poems called the Roman Odes form a cycle, and must be approached with that in mind. First, evidence external to the six poems, namely their position in the three books of Odes, was adduced to suggest their status as sequence, and second, internal references, balances and echoes in the sequence itself also were seen to suggest a cycle of poems, as does identity of meter and fluidity of poem boundaries. The object of study was all this, not merely the words on the page.

The object of study was also, implicitly, the lyric form itself as practiced by this poet. Thus we assumed with periodic exceptions that the reader had "read" the corpus of Odes I-III, that is, was a competent reader of Latin lyric in these meters, with their Greek antecedents and Latin relatives in the lyric form, largely unnoted here. This object of study was not illuminated in the scale practiced for the Horatian texts because it would have been cumbersome to begin *ab ovo* and because in reality people do not read (or read about) lyric poems on this level of complexity unless they already have some idea of the form, which the critic can take for granted just as the poet does.

Although not explicitly stated as such while the critical process was underway, this act of criticism on the extrinsic level implicitly assigned a teleological function and purpose to the Roman Odes: to form a new perspective on the world of around 23 B.C., the opportunities and dangers for ruler, institution of the state, family and individual citizen. Didactic in the highest sense of the word, the poem sequence functions to provide understanding of this new juncture of Roman development, but also to influence change. The Roman gods, the Roman state and the Roman family are presented as interlocked in a new way, with great positive potential if certain attitudes are maintained: attitudes the poet identifies and inculcates in his art. On the archaeological level, it can now be asserted that the foregoing reading of the Roman Odes assigns lyric a new function; the source and origin of this development of lyric into monumental sequence of civic poetry cannot be discovered in antecedent poetry shaping or determining Horace's achievement. This is not to say that a very fruitful line of inquiry cannot be opened up seeking to link the Roman Odes to Horace's other poetry, or to other poetry in Latin, such as the common concerns of the Roman Odes and the *Aeneid*, or the ironic exploitation of them by Propertius' elegies, III.1-5. Further, weighty studies have been undertaken linking Horace to Homer, Alcaeus, Pindar, Callimachus, Theocritus and others, and relating his poetry to Catullus, Vergil, Statius, Prudentius, and others. But it is not the function of the present work of criticism to undertake such explorations in detail for the Roman Odes; in seeking to read them, it is simply not necessary to be conscious of each potential connection. Horace's grammar of conventions can be adequately learned through reading Horace: an extreme statement, but one necessary to maintaining the critical perspective here embraced.

On the historical level, compensation has perhaps been made for not dwelling on archaeological "source and origin" studies. For the critical study just completed obviously makes a special effort to relate the poem-cycle as event to other non-literary events: political, social, religious and visual. Most of the foregoing pages devoted to intrinsic or descriptive criticism are yoked to this extrinsic mode of historical analysis. Horace's making six lyric poems (with their antecedent and subsequent relatives in his corpus) into a cycle results in monumentalizing the lyric form and in assigning it a new function, thus providing a new object of study and thus raising new teleological and archaeological questions that have been illuminated here largely in terms of a non-literary historical entity, the Roman historical relief.

The assumptions behind this choice can now conveniently be set forth. An urban complex society like that of 23 B.C. is capable of being trained to read an urban complex poetry, as modern criticism of Horace's and Vergil's poetic corpus so amply reveals. These reading acts were performed by an audience that likewise read inscriptions on coins and on monuments, and further experienced in controlled sequential style highly conventional signs called historical reliefs. It is no exaggeration to say that they "read" these the way they were expected to read poetry: by establishing context, grasping the network of conventions, and by reading back and forth to achieve valid interpretation. Horace's poetry of process is analogous to the process of reading a monument. Horace has thus expanded radically the use of the institution of the lyric into the realm of civic monument.

Both extrinsic and intrinsic critical operations combined to work out these foregoing interpretations of the Roman Odes. Literary competence was incrementally gained as the reader moved from the expected and the known through the cycle perceived as something unexpected and unknown. The poet pulls no surprises, however, on the attentive reader. Rather, Horace continuously creates for us a poetics by which we are enabled to understand the Roman Odes, his willed intent, and the conventions of this extension of the institution of lyric poetry. By making central himself, by canalizing the reader's expectations and reactions and by facilitating certain readings back and forth in the sequence (and in the whole corpus of Odes I-III) the poet teaches the reader how to make sense of the text by watching what the text does (and does not do) to the reader. Thus the stable conclusiveness of the gnome of decay, at the very end of the cycle, is not necessarily to be perceived as the stopping point of the cycle's artistic impact; closure is achieved at the end of the cycle, but closure is not the poet's final view of the Roman world; it is rather a way of finishing the artistic structure that bodies forth "a way out" of the spiral of decay and decline. Horace has reliably and consistently presented to the competent reader meeting him half-way on the continuum of literary institution and convention a sense of the structure of the Roman Odes: a structure we have tried to illuminate in terms of an analogous structure such as the *Ara Pacis Augustae* without suggesting that this was ever in the mind of Horace or of any Augustan.

The Roman Odes seen from this point of view are very much a part of the new Augustan rhetoric and aesthetic that purveyed a moral imitation of the values and practices of heroes of the Roman past rather than relied on Greek models. The format of the Temple and Forum of Mars Ultor alone shows Augustan preoccupation with marshalling heroes from Rome's early days into a programmatic statement of present values and ideas. Augustus' own supreme position was based (in theory) on his functioning as patron with his clients throughout the world, but he had in Julius Caesar ample precedent for functioning as a divine ruler as well. More radical still than Divus Julius, than Antony or any of the other adversaries that one by one fell by the wayside as he progressively assigned new meaning to the old institutions of the proconsular imperium and the tribunician power, Augustus wrapped his new departures in the old traditions of the Roman gods, state and family. Horace's Roman Odes are but one objectification of this excogitated policy.

That the poet perceived his age as one wherein new departures were best disguised within old forms need surprise no one familiar with the Roman bent for conservative values. But unlike Augustus' military autocracy carefully concealed within Republican institutions, Horace's

new poetic venture borrowed only the outward forms of lyric meter to set
forth a new, imaginative and personal art form: the monumental civic
lyric sequence. Its radical and romantic appeal can still be felt even if its
programmatic elements are as inert as the silent faces gazing past us from
some frieze. Horace in his Roman Odes like Augustus in the new state
binds himself to the Roman tradition, assigns new meaning to the old
forms, and constitutes a lasting monument of a high order. He mediates
the ethos of the emperor consorting with the gods, and the pathos of the
Roman soldier repelling enemies threatening Rome herself. But unlike
Augustus, that greatest of persuaders in the ancient world, Horace ended
up not persuading himself all the time, as the reader of the many lyrics
that do not deal with Roman questions, and of the *Epistles* in particular,
knows. Perhaps in ordering his books for publication Horace wished to
send some such signal about there being another world where too he had
talent to live, and hence juxtaposed to the solemn civic monument of the
Roman Odes the personal, romantic text of Odes III.7, "Quid fles,
Asterie?"

> Quid fles, Asterie, quem tibi candidi
> primo restituent vere Favonii
>   Thyna merce beatum,
>   constantis iuvenem fide
>
> Gygen? ille Notis actus ad Oricum   5
> post insana Caprae sidera frigidas
>   noctis non sine multis
>   insomnis lacrimis agit.
>
> atqui sollicitae nuntius hospitae,
> suspirare Chloen et miseram tuis   10
>   dicens ignibus uri,
>   Temptat mille vafer modis.
>
> ut Proetum mulier perfida credulum
> falsis inpulerit criminibus nimis
>   casto Bellerophontae   15
>   maturare necem refert,
>
> narrat paene datum Pelea Tartaro,
> Magnessam Hippolyten dum fugit abstinens,
>   et peccare docentis
>   fallax historias movet—   20

frustra: nam scopulis surdior Icari
voces audit adhuc integer. at tibi
   ne vicinus Enipeus
      plus iusto placeat cave,

quamvis non alius flectere equum sciens   25
aeque conspicitur gramine Martio
   nec quisquam citus aeque
      Tusco denatat alveo.

prima nocte domum claude neque in vias
sub cantu querulae despice tibiae,   30
   et te saepe vocanti
      duram difficilis mane.

Why weep, Asterie, for a man whom cloudfree western breezes will restore to you at spring's arrival: (2) Gyges, rich with Bithynian merchandise, a young man of unwavering faith. Driven by southern gales to take refuge at Oricus after the rising of Capra's mad stars, he passes chilly nights sleepless, with many a tear. (3) And yet—word comes from his restless hostess, saying that Chloe sighs and is desperately aflame for him, your lover; and slyly she woos him in a thousand fashions. (4) Her messenger recounts how a faithless woman incited Proetus, trusting her false accusations, to send to an early death Bellerophon who was too chaste. (5) He tells the story of Peleus almost sent to hell, when, fleeing, he resisted Hippolyte of Magnesia; and he deceptively draws attention to stories that counsel sin—(6) in vain: for more unheeding than Icarus' crags he hears the blandishments, up to now uncorrupted. But for yourself, watch out that neighbor Enipeus not find with you favor greater than is right, (7) though no one else is discerned on Mars' field so skilful in sitting his horse, nor does anyone so swift swim down the Tuscan channel. (8) At night's arrival close up your house, and do not look down into the street at the onset of that wavering flute; even if he repeatedly calls you cruel, remain obdurate.

INDEX

Printed in the United States
By Bookmasters